THE
GARDEN
FARMER

THE
GARDEN FARMER

FRANCINE RAYMOND

◨ SQUARE PEG

CONTENTS

What could be nicer than

a meal packed with ingredients

you've grown yourself?

The freshest salad leaves, perfectly ripe tomatoes, an omelette from your own birds, even home-reared sausages; finished with some juicy berries and eaten on a table in the garden jollied with a bunch of homegrown flowers – all produce from your own small plot.

Gardens extend our lives beyond the boundaries of our house's four walls, and I'm a great believer in making that little bit more of outside space. Some of us garden to show off artistic fantasies, others to create our own little bit of paradise, and a few just to improve the view from the house. It's a full-time job to some busy smallholders, while to others who energetically mow their lawns at weekends it's an occasional burst of exercise.

I garden to hold tight to my connection with the outside world. It lightens my mood and keeps me sane, improves my health and gives me hope – a small patch of soil that's mine, where I follow age-old rituals and make things grow, just like that first child's plot or indoor garden at nursery school.

The results may not be self-sufficiency – just a larder packed with small tastes of the season, tiny flavours to heighten the senses; smells that evoke souvenirs of good times; and flowery visions to cheer, all at peak freshness straight from the plot. And it's fun to share this harvest month-by-month with friends and family.

Most of us live in towns and cities with little outside space and it's a battle to keep in touch with the seasons and celebrate those seasonal delights that augur special times of the year. They give us something to look forward to, the thrill of new flavours and the satisfaction of harvest, however meagre.

I grow a few essential vegetables to taste the season: those first eagerly expected delicacies, the gluts of high summer and supplies of salad throughout the year. My herbs add spice to life, and since moving to Kent's Garden of England I've concentrated on growing fruit. I love the blossom, the excitement of fruit ripening and the chance to eat it straight from the tree.

You need bees to pollinate fruit, and I'm keen to encourage early bumblebees to kick-start baskets of cherries and apricots, and other bees and butterflies. So, even though I'm not expecting honey, providing year-round flowers brim-full of nectar and a welcoming habitat is part of my gardening year.

Poultry-keeping has been my passion for a quarter of a century. My hens eat pests and leftovers, and in return improve the soil and produce the freshest eggs for the kitchen. Ducks, geese and other poultry are just as productive, and if you have the space, maybe even a couple of pigs. I love the companionship of gardening with my flock, the glamour and drama of their adventures.

So let's decorate our houses with flowers on high days and holidays, and celebrate those occasions outside with garden parties or by just relaxing in the fresh air. Life's pleasures are made of simple transient moments, so let's share our plot's produce with friends, family and wildlife, and make the most of our gardens.

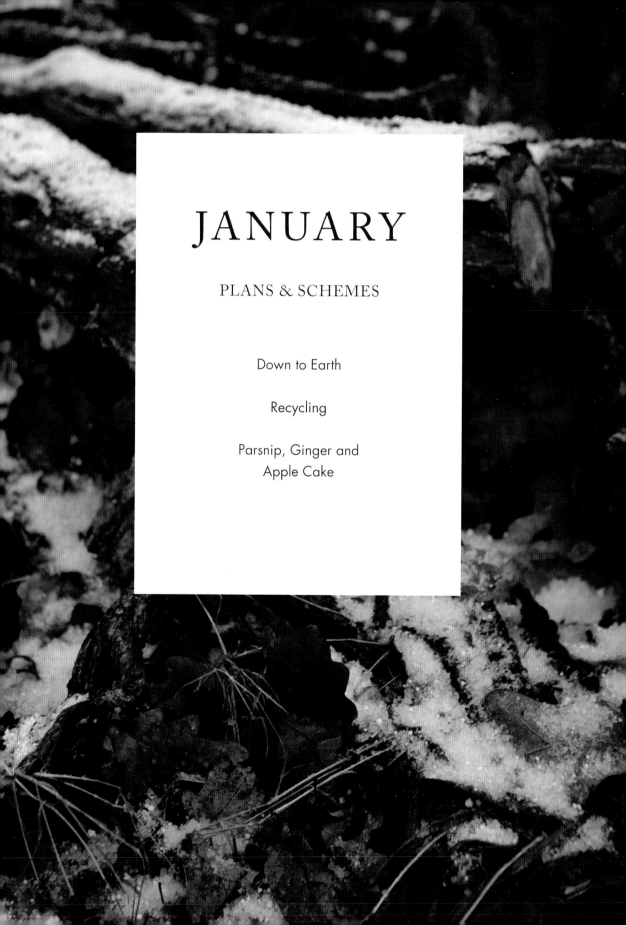

JANUARY

PLANS & SCHEMES

Down to Earth

Recycling

Parsnip, Ginger and
Apple Cake

A new gardening year, and it's time to take stock, make plans and build up strength for the coming months.

L ike our dormant plants, hibernating wildlife and warming soil, we need a period of vernalisation too, to re-energise and kick-start a year of growth and creativity. And where better to start January than the fireside, surrounded by the new season's seed catalogues, a few scribbled garden plans, a cup of something fortifying and a piece of cake?

It's time to ask ourselves: what exactly are gardens for? My younger son suggested 'chilling, relaxing and having fun'; the older one wanted space for his children to play and somewhere to eat; friends chipped in with somewhere to grow food, to design a vista, and to make a sanctuary – a place to escape, to exercise or be self-sufficient. For me it's food,

fun and a fantasy world where I battle with the weather to create a haven for myself and my family, for animals, my plants and local wildlife.

Take a look out of an upstairs window and examine the bare bones of your garden. Do you need to make changes? Now's the time, when everything slumbers, to rejuvenate, edit and change direction. Learn from past experience: was the table too far from the cooking area last year? Did you grow too much of one thing and not nearly enough of another? Is there too much shade, or more shelter needed? Did your gardening ambitions exhaust you or would it be fun to have more growing space?

Even in an established garden, there's nothing more invigorating than a new plan – a slight change that will open views, challenge perceptions or solve problems. Perhaps you'd like to grow more flowers for the house, widen your vegetable repertoire, make a new herb garden, keep bees or poultry, or even pigs? Or maybe you would like to go off on a tangent and grow a crop of mushrooms or cultivate edible snails?

If you are growing vegetables, remember that you'll need to rotate your beds to avoid diseases taking hold, and soil deficiencies developing. The best bet is to have four separate beds and to grow different crops each year in each bed. Vegetables can be divided into four groups:

Brassicas: Brussels sprouts, cabbage, kales and radishes
Legumes: peas, broad beans and all other sorts of beans
Onions: garlic, leeks, shallots and onions
Roots: beetroot, carrots, fennel, parsley, celeriac and other root crops

A further bed where you can permanently grow perennial vegetables like rhubarb, artichokes and cardoons would be useful if you have the space, but I grow these at the back of all my beds and leave them in situ as their compatriots move on each year.

Some veg, like salads, all the pumpkins and courgettes and sweetcorn, are less fussy and can be grown wherever they'll fit. You could also pop your veg into your flowerbeds, or grow tomatoes and peppers in containers.

Take a look at the new season's seed catalogues and see if there are temptations: stimulating new colours, cheering fragrances and reviving tastes to try. Perhaps you took seeds and cuttings from plants you coveted in friends' gardens? If not, promise to do so this year. Make a resolution to get more colour, scent and excitement into your borders and place your seed order now.

Do you have the space and time to take up a new hobby? Maybe really fresh eggs would be a welcome addition. Just a few hens, ducks or geese will enrich your life as well as your compost, and widen your menu. Would you like to encourage more wildlife into your garden, especially pollinating insects? If so, create a more welcoming habitat and beneficial food for them.

Even if you're entirely satisfied, the garden will be moving on, needing fresh energy and new heart, so it's the right time to add compost, mulches, soil conditioners and natural fertilisers to the soil. There's plenty to do outside on sunny days to re-energise both you and your garden and make this coming year the best yet.

Resolutions

- To try to get out in the garden for an hour or so every day.

- To edit existing schemes and repeat those that were successful.

- To water and feed containers before they desperately need it.

- To start fewer schemes but finish more.

- To take care of my gardening equipment better.

- To sit around in the garden with a cup of something more often.

Down to Earth

WHILE THE GARDEN SLUMBERS, and you have the time, think about the bare bones and basic materials. A garden is as good as its soil, and now is a good time to add mulches to improve its texture and fecundity.

Every day I go out into my garden and become a magician. I take kitchen and garden waste, and hey presto – turn them into crumbly compost. It's one of the most satisfying things about the process of gardening and appeals to the penny-pinching puritan in my soul. How we recycle waste effectively is one of the gardener's biggest quandaries. A whole section of my garden is dedicated to this black art – a hidden coven where benevolent spells are concocted for the greater good of my plants.

Compost Heaps

Out of sight, at the bottom of my garden, under the canopy of a great oak, I've made a dead hedge in the gap between fence and compost heaps. Here, branches too small to burn and too big to compost rot slowly away, hopefully offering sanctuary to beneficial insects in the meantime. Backing on to it comes a row of pallet bays, where kitchen and garden waste – a careful balance between green and brown matter (see adjacent column) – decompose slowly throughout the year, enriched with and activated by home-produced chicken manure and bedding. There are as many ways to compost as there are cake recipes. Mine has been perfected to deal with my waste over decades of trial and error. I don't have to turn my compost because it has been cooking for a whole year, with just the right balance of materials in a shady spot that helps to keep temperatures constant. I also use other methods that provide extra material for my garden.

BUILDERS' BAGS

Packed close to the compost heaps are a couple of open-weave builders' bags: one of gently composting leaves swept up from lawns and paths, and the other crammed with rotting woodchip

COMPOSTING MATERIALS

Aim for two-thirds carbon-rich brown content to a third nitrogen-rich greens.

Brown
Straw and hay
Sawdust and woodchip
Shredded newsprint and
    cardboard
Dry leaves, stems and twigs
Cotton and woolly rags

Green
Grass and soft leafy growth
Fruit and veg
Pet bedding and hair
Uncooked kitchen waste
Coffee grounds and teabags
Flowers and crushed
    eggshells

and sawdust from the tree surgeon's visit. Oak, chestnut and sycamore leaves take over a year to rot down; it helps to break them down by running a mower over them, but small leaves like ash and elder rot more quickly. Next to these I keep a neat pile of sodden cardboard and a covered bag of wood ash from my wood-burning stove, both of which I layer on the compost heaps.

COMPOSTERS

A vermin-proof aerobic composter takes pride of place in my compost battery. There to put pay to food waste, it will compost 32 times faster than a conventional heap. Mine is a Hotbin, the size of an elegant black wheelie bin, which needs no turning and reaches temperatures of 60°C. To achieve these temperatures, you need to feed the bacteria and give them oxygen by layering kitchen and garden waste with bulking agents: woodchip, shredded paper and cardboard. My only problem is a lack of leftovers, so I've requisitioned my son's family's binful every week.

This is the working heart of my garden.

BOKASHI BINS

For those who want to compost food but have less space, the Bokashi system may be the answer. This is Japanese bran that pickles food waste in a small container (32 x 32 x 37cm) kept under the kitchen sink. Simply scrape your leftovers into the bin, sprinkle on a handful of bran and seal the lid. A few weeks later the compost can be added to your heap or used as mulch on the soil. A liquid is also produced that makes a nutritious plant feed.

WORMERIES

You could also try a wormery. These come in a range of different sizes and consist of composting trays with holes. As the worms eat the waste, it loses its volume – from cabbage to sprout-sized – and the worms climb to the next level, leaving behind a rich vermicompost to be used in the garden. Worms can be fussy eaters though, and often balk at bones, garlic, spicy food, eggs, dairy, salt and oil.

Animal Manures

Most soils can be improved by adding organic manure – it adds nourishment and substance to sandy soils and lightens clay ones. Always leave to compost between layers of brown and green waste, and never apply fresh. Animal excrement, added to their hair and feathers, plus litter and bedding, especially straw, hemp, corrugated card or shredded paper, is powerful stuff. Avoid wood shavings and sawdust, as they're often treated with preservative and take too long to rot down.

Horse and cow manures are the most valuable, especially as a soil conditioner, but should be kept under cover as they lose value when wet. Goat and sheep manures are richer in nitrogen. Horse manure can contain weed seeds.

Pig manure must be composted to a high heat and turned regularly. Mix with brown composting materials and turn once a month, then leave to compost over winter until spring, when it's ready to use.

Poultry manure is highest in nitrogen and phosphorus and

My veg beds slumbering under a duvet of snow.

these nutrients are readily available to plants. It should be stored in a dry place, then layered in your heap. Avoid manure from intensively farmed birds, and never use fresh because it will burn plants. Outdoor-raised birds' droppings may contain weed seeds.

Rotted seaweed is nearly as beneficial as farmyard manure: it's lower in phosphates, but richer in potash and makes a good soil conditioner. You'll need permission from the owner of the foreshore to collect it (often the local council). It doesn't need washing, just add it to your compost heap in layers.

The Annual Mulch

In mid-winter I assemble all the different elements and cast my spells. On a large tarpaulin, I mix year-old garden compost (emptying the heap ready for the new year's offerings) with dark leaf-mould, a little woodchip with grit and occasionally some composted cow manure bought from the local garden centre. I aim to mulch all my beds as part of the great garden spring clean.

Then, because I live in the balmy south and my beds are already warming up, I spread a cosy 5cm layer on all raised beds, vegetable and soft fruit plots, and around my fruit trees, leaving a gap around stems and trunks. I rescue any self-sown seedlings that I want to save, and top up any large pots and containers with mulch; the smaller ones will be fed with a liquid seaweed mixture at fortnightly intervals from March onwards.

This mulch will act as a weed suppressant (though however long I bake my compost it always seems to grow a moss of tiny seedlings – easily hoed off as they first appear) and will improve my thick yellow clay soil's texture, while helping to retain winter's moisture in the soil. Now, my plants will kick off the new season in the best of spirits.

ESSENTIAL VEG

If you're dying to get your food crops started, broad beans can be sown now.

- Sow seeds in small 7cm pots and keep them in a light frost-free place.
- Harden them off before planting out when they're 15cm tall.
- Pinch out their growing tips when the first beans appear – you can use these in salads.
- Stake and keep an eye open for blackfly.
- Harvest pods when the beans are medium sized and not floury.
- If you like them, keep a few beans to dry and sow next year.

Recycling

Gᴀʀᴅᴇɴɪɴɢ ᴏɴ ᴀ sʜᴏᴇsᴛʀɪɴɢ is an art, and compost, pots and seeds are some of the gardener's regular outgoings that can be most readily economised on.

Seed-saving is a great way to cut down overheads and since your parent plants will have already adapted to your growing conditions, success is guaranteed.

Throughout the harvest season, mark interesting non-hybrid varieties and plants you love with string and collect the ripe seed late on a sunny day before winter weather takes its toll. Pop them into labelled envelopes. Dry them in an airy place until completely desiccated, then crumble the pods and winnow the seeds to separate them from the chaff.

Some seeds, like cucumbers and aubergines, need to be collected from the fruit, so scoop them out into a bowl of water. The seeds will sink. Rinse them in a sieve and leave them to dry on a plate, then store in jars. Tomatoes, melons and squash must

Outside plants are dormant while inside seeds are waiting to be planted.

be fermented to remove their germination-inhibiting coating. Put these into a jam jar and leave in a warm place until bubbles appear on the surface, drain, then clean as above. Store all seeds in a rodent-proof box until planting time.

There are other ways of creatively saving money. I'm a passionate boot-fair trawler. At the crack of dawn on a Sunday morning when most sensible people are enjoying a lie-in, I'm trudging a municipal car park or some farmer's muddy field, looking for bric-a-brac and gardenalia.

I pass by the mountains of baby clothes, the stacks of DVDs and vinyl, and the plastic toys on my way to the dealers who look as though they've emptied their garages, where I can find buckets and pans, old tin baths, and anything to pot plants in. Unusual planters like old chimney pots, stone sinks and metal farmyard feeds are available to the eagle-eyed, at a price.

TIMELY ADVICE

Order your seeds early from catalogues.

Keep pollinating insects in mind when ordering flower seeds (see page 61).

Mulch rhubarb crowns and pop one under a cloche to force.

Aim to have some plants in flower year-round for the house (see pages 104–114).

Bring in pots of forced bulbs and leave them in appropriate places.

If you're planning to keep poultry or pigs, book a course.

Plan to prune fruit trees while they're dormant.

Wait until March to prune cherries.

But others are dirt-cheap. It's not just the rock-bottom prices that appeal: I'm a master at make-do-and-mend, and love the thrill of the hunt. Over the past twenty years, I've found galvanised metal drawers (perfect for my alpines), enamel baking pans (ideal for my succulents), and a collection of buckets that do well as cache-pots for back-door plants, like salvias and bulbs. I have an old tin bath full of beautiful blue muscari that I'll soon move into place by my porch to flower.

Since all these plants need good drainage, I make holes in the bases of new containers using a hefty Phillips screwdriver and mallet, cushioning my 'find' on the lawn. Some are painted using metal primer followed by topcoats from cycle and car shops.

Dealers who specialise in old tools are a good source of ladies'-weight spades, and builders' barrows, wooden ladders and old shelves to convert into plant stands are common, but *caveat emptor*. Watering cans should be held up to the light to check for leaks.

There's plenty of choice when it comes to garden furniture, too, though mostly in the white plastic department – which is irredeemable. But old deckchairs are good finds and can be easily re-covered by tacking on new lengths of canvas. Second-hand cushions can be re-covered to soften hard wooden benches, while old rugs, blankets and Indian bedspreads can be picked up really cheaply to use as awnings and tablecloths.

Car boot sales usually boast a few plant stalls as well. Some are genuine nurseries, others buy up plants at wholesale markets to re-sell, and then there are stallholders who pot up their leftovers and flog them with their household effects. Use your discretion and maybe re-pot with new compost after a short period in isolation.

Parsnip, Ginger and Apple Cake

Pure comfort food, using apples and parsnips from the plot.

Preheat the oven to 180°C/gas 4.

Cream together 170g each of butter and muscovado sugar.

Add half a grated apple and 170g of finely grated parsnip.

Sift in 350g of flour, a pinch of baking powder, and a teaspoon each of cinnamon and nutmeg, then add a sprinkle of sultanas and chopped preserved ginger and combine.

Add 4 beaten eggs gradually.

Pour in a tablespoon of cider vinegar, 120ml of water and a teaspoon of vanilla essence.

Transfer to a buttered 20cm lined cake tin and decorate with the other half of the apple, sliced into rounds or half-moons.

Bake in the oven for just over an hour.

Brush the surface of the warm cake with diluted jam and serve with cinnamon-dusted crème fraîche.

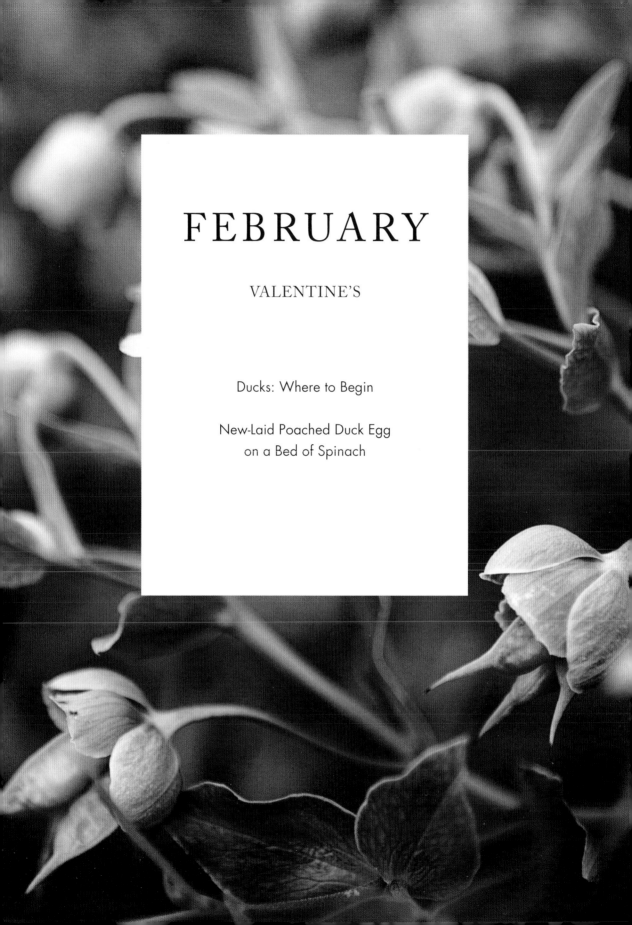

FEBRUARY

VALENTINE'S

Ducks: Where to Begin

New-Laid Poached Duck Egg
on a Bed of Spinach

Look carefully: there are small
signs of life in the winter garden,
optimistically heralding spring.

Gently rake back winter's mulch of leaves and you'll find emerald bulb shoots, modest wildflowers and pretty foliage. Some sweet-smelling shrubs and trees are flowering bravely to catch the early pollinators. Vegetable gardening can be tentatively started under cover, in the greenhouse or under cloches. Windowsills everywhere are home to pans of seedlings, but don't start them too early or they'll get straggly.

Bring in a bunch of February's blooms – you'll be surprised at what's on offer: delicate pink cherry blossom, fragrant sweet box, winter-flowering clematis, daphnes, hellebores, mahonia and euphorbias for colour and fragrance. Add structure with pussy willow or budding birch twigs and more perfume with rosemary branches.

Together they'll make a welcome bunch to cheer the house or a ravishing bouquet to give someone special on Valentine's day, especially if you speak lovingly in the language of flowers.

Love is in the air in the garden: mid-February is the start of the new season, birds start to pair up, insects appear briefly on pale sunny days and spring is nearly sprung. My leafless oak tree is home to a squirm of squirrels who don't seem to hibernate and instead fly through its branches, mating, fighting and chattering.

Ducks seem to have the best of all worlds. They can walk (or waddle) and swim and fly. They are endlessly entertaining to watch in any of these elements, and many of us will have fed them from our pushchairs in the park or at the

village pond. I bet the word 'duck' features high on the list of babies' first words.

Twenty-five years ago, with these memories in mind, we excavated a pond in our garden in Suffolk. Planting up the banks with indigenous wildflowers, we built a pontoon so our sons could lie on their tummies and watch the wildlife. We were entranced as a mallard duck and her eleven ducklings made their home among the lily pads.

We watched them grow like wildfire and thankfully disappear during autumn to join the flock on the village pond. Imagine our horror the following spring when those eleven fat mallard reappeared with mates and had similar success bringing up their offspring. You can guess the rest. Within a couple of years our garden was awash with inhabitants that turned our watery idyll into a duck pond.

Voyeurs to their lurid love lives, we woke every morning to their raucous dawn chorus, raised their orphans and struggled to feed them all, but I still love ducks best of all poultry – they're adorable time-wasters. And of course, there is an easier, painless way to keep a controllable flock of ducks in a smallish garden and enjoy their eggs as well.

Ducks: Where to Begin

WOULD YOU LIKE a regular supply of rich and delicious eggs, fantastic pest control and a flock of charming co-gardeners? Then try a few ducks. All you need is a little common sense and to stick to a few basic principles.

In most circumstances you don't need permission to keep poultry in your garden, but check your house deeds or rental agreement to make sure, then speak to neighbours to see if they'll duck-sit your flock when you're on holiday and are prepared to put up with the odd quack. If everyone's happy, decide where to site your run and pond – somewhere that offers shade from the sun and shelter from the wind, as spacious and secure as possible.

On to expense. Pure-breed ducks cost more than other poultry, especially the ornamentals, so stick to the less exotic breeds to start with. Your duck house can cost as much or as little as you want, but buy or build one large enough for you to feed them in and you'll have no trouble getting them in at night. Feed costs are similar to other poultry, depending on how free-range your flock is. Before you set out with any new livestock venture, consider all the costs and make a plan that you will be able to afford.

As with all poultry, most breeds were developed to lay eggs or bred for the table. Then the showmen got hold of them and exaggerated their physical idiosyncrasies. It's best to go for utility strains – not highly-bred show birds, unless you're prepared to give them five-star treatment – and choose one of the flightless breeds unless you want to clip wings annually. Go to local poultry shows and scan smallholding magazines and websites. The Domestic Waterfowl Club will provide lists of breeders. Always visit before buying and give yourself plenty of time to order – you may have to wait for eggs to hatch and ducklings to grow.

Where to Keep Your Ducks

I'd never keep ducks without a pond. You'll come across advice that they only need enough to dunk their heads, but anyone who has seen how ducks take to water will be unable to deny them.

Ducks will happily make their home in your garden, especially if it includes a pond.

Remember, though, that even a shallow pond can be dangerous to small children, so make sure the whole area is securely fenced.

The ideal duck home is a netted area (of at least 2 square metres per bird), with a shed, a pond and gate leading to occasional access to your garden – depending on their security and how fussy a gardener you are. Keep them in a covered area for the first couple of weeks until they know their address. Smaller breeds (and Muscovies, which fly well despite their bulk) will need the flight feathers of one wing trimmed (see page 45), but watch your breeder do this first.

A simple fence 1 metre high will keep your birds in, but won't keep predators out, so a fox-proof run 2 metres high with a roof and a wire apron to stop predators digging in is best. Cut away any overhanging branches that might offer overhead springboard entry. Foxes patrol their territories every night, so make sure you shut both run and house every evening without fail.

Ducks are hardy. House them for easy egg collection and for protection from foxes, dogs and mink, rather than keeping warm. They'll need an area just over half a metre square per bird with above-head ventilation, and they sleep on the floor, not perching like hens. An ordinary 8' x 4' garden shed will be fine for 6 to 8 ducks. Build a couple of 30cm square nest boxes lined with straw in a dark corner.

The floor should be kept dry, with corrugated cardboard bedding, straw or even dried leaves, but this will need changing often. Ducks are easy to keep, but very messy, so regular housekeeping is a must – an easy chore for such delightful co-gardeners. Make sure the front door is large enough for your ducks (a hen house pop-hole won't do), and consider the entrance, as most prefer a ramp to waddle up rather than steps.

If you are building a concrete pond, make it 30cm deep, to be easily cleaned with a broom and running hose, or use a simple fibreglass garden pond or children's sandpit. Change the water regularly, often daily. If it becomes really dirty, it will be high in nitrogen, so don't pour it on your plants, but siphon it onto your compost heap. A large pond with an island house may seem a good idea, but remember: foxes can swim and walk on ice, and you'll need daily access.

If you're excavating a pond, use a strong butyl liner and protect its edges with flints, or concrete paving, otherwise your flock will enlarge its diameters with constant dabbling. Our pond somehow survived despite its hundreds of inhabitants and verdant green contents.

Finally, ducks need shade, so put up bamboo screens if there are no available trees or shrubs. In winter, bank up strategically placed straw bales for extra shelter in the run.

Choosing Your Ducks

All domestic ducks evolved from wild mallard that were then developed into different breeds. Occasionally, pure black and white 'sports' occurred, too, and were bred for their looks or lighter meat. Others were developed for their laying potential – Khaki Campbells lay almost an egg a day, more than most pure-breed hens. Heavy breeds like the Aylesbury were obviously destined for the table, while the more decorative birds were bred as ornamentals or decoys for sport. Muscovies are a separate species, probably more closely related to geese.

Aylesbury

My rainbow tribe was made up of mallard escapees from a local game farm, interbred over the years with Campbells, Call Ducks and other breeds unaccountably left on our drive – unforgivably mixed as far as purists are concerned, but prodigiously willing and able to reproduce without shelter, and like most natural hybrids, their vigour was legendary.

Starting from scratch, I'd buy a mature pure-breed trio – a drake and two ducks – and then hatch out some ducklings in the following years to bring your flock up to numbers your garden and pond can cope with. A small garden would be fine with just two ducks. Unlike cockerels, drakes get on quite well together, but don't have too many or your ducks will be pestered.

Both drakes and ducks live for about eight years. In some breeds they look similar, the male just a little bigger with a couple of curled tail feathers; in others that have mallard in their make-up, the sexes look totally different. Only ducks quack; drakes make a *basso*, rasping croak.

Black East Indian

If you have a small garden and little appetite for eggs (or duck *à l'orange*), I can recommend the bantam breeds or tiny Call Ducks, known in Holland as *Kwackers*. They come in lots of different colours and patterns and lay well. Their only drawback is a really irritating quack that starts at 4 a.m. in the summer.

AYLESBURY (UK) 4.5kg
Pure white with a pinkish bill, orange legs and webs, perfected over centuries as a table bird. Deep-keeled and with a low-slung undercarriage in show birds, which should be avoided. Too heavy to fly, lays about 100 white eggs a year and will breed if not too fat.

Call Duck

BLACK EAST INDIAN (USA) 900g
A tiny ornamental with lustrous beetle-green sheen, smart matching black legs and webs. A garden forager, so goodbye to slugs and snails. Will fly, so wing-clipping needed. Lays unusual slate grey to black eggs, fading to blue. Expensive.

CALL DUCK (UK) under 900g
Dear little things, firm and cobby with a round head and constant irritating quack that was used to lure wildfowl to shoots. Comes in a rainbow of pretty colours, lays well and eats grass. A good garden bird, causing little damage and mess.

Campbell

CAMPBELL (UK) 2.2kg
Bred in 1900 by a Mrs Campbell for eggs – sometimes more than 300 a year. Slim and active birds with sloping carriage. The khaki-coloured ones are the most productive, but they are also available in white and dark.

INDIAN RUNNER (INDIA) 2.2kg
Brought to the UK by a Scots sea captain in 1850. Good layers of greenish-white eggs with an upright consort's stance that will forage in the garden. They can't fly, so walk quickly and need a stress-free environment. Available in fawn, white, black and chocolate.

Indian Runner

MUSCOVY (S. AMERICA) male 5.5kg – female 2.75kg
The drake is bigger than the duck, with a knobby head, and will

fight other drakes. The ducks don't quack. Good parents and egg-sitters. Need plenty of space and fly well. They lay 180 eggs a year and will produce three broods. Fine dual-purpose birds.

PEKIN (CHINA) 3.6kg

A creamy white duck with canary-yellow legs and bill that's slimmer than the white Aylesbury. Very good layers of white eggs. Friendly, inquisitive, flightless birds with soft eyes and useful in the garden, where they forage and swim.

Muscovy

ROUEN (FRANCE) 4.5kg

Looks like a very fat mallard. Largest breed, bred unsurprisingly for the table. Has a majestic bulk, but don't let them get overweight, and allow plenty of opportunity for exercise. Lays a clutch of greenish eggs.

What to Feed Your Ducks

Basically, ducks need water, grit, grass and food. Like hens, they are omnivores, and left to their own devices in a large garden will balance their needs with just a mixed corn meal morning and evening. Kept in a run, they need a diet of corn and protein pellets (don't give them mash because ducks turn everything to mash). This will be supplemented with insects (and you hope slugs and snails from the garden) and grass from their surroundings. Kitchen waste is no longer allowed as a feedstuff, but garden leftovers will be greedily gobbled up.

Pekin

Offer feed in a metal hopper for 20 minutes a day in their shed, morning and evening. If you want eggs, feed 20% corn to 80% pellets. Keep the area around their food clean, and make sure there's drinking water at all times. Grit is available naturally in your garden, but must be supplied to help them digest their food if ducks are confined to their pen.

Adopt a routine. Feed your birds in their house, then let them out into their run or safely into the garden to potter until sunset, when supper is served in their quarters and they're shut up for the night.

Ducks' bills enable them to pick up food quite delicately, or to dabble and sieve food by sucking in water. They'll eat weeds, seeds, grass cuttings, brassica leaves and snails, and enjoy

Rouen

finishing off fallen fruit in an orchard, especially after it has started to ferment.

Keep all your feed in a galvanised bin with a metal lid to prevent rats sharing, and make sure leftovers are removed at night.

Duck Eggs

Duck eggs used to be unpopular. Historic rumours of salmonella (probably due to their shells being more porous and less long-life than hens' eggs) have taken their toll, but recent 'cheffy' endorsements are bringing them deservedly back onto the menu. Eat them fresh. Most ducks lay in the morning, so collect and wipe clean immediately. Discard any you find lying in the run or laid in the garden or pond to discourage vermin and broodiness. Don't eat these, as you won't know how fresh they are.

White ducks lay white eggs and so do Runners; the rest lay blue or greenish-tinted ones. Duck eggs are great for cooking – especially for baking or for rich and creamy scrambled eggs. Eat them before they are a week old. Ducks lay well for three years

Feed your ducks well, and they'll produce lots of eggs in season for the kitchen.

or so, then gradually lay less each year. You don't need a drake for your ducks to lay, only for them to produce fertile eggs.

Augmenting Your Flock

Ducks are gregarious, and introducing newcomers is easy. Just make sure they're kept under cover for a fortnight until they get used to their new home, or they'll fly off. Young birds without a mum to support them will need to be segregated in separate lodgings until they're fully grown, but hatching your own is the most natural way to increase your stock.

Drakes need to have been kept with ducks for a month to be sure eggs are fertile, so if you don't already have one in your flock, add him a little while before you are hoping to produce. Increase the percentage of pellets to grain for the ladies, but drakes need little encouragement. They are legendarily promiscuous, indulging in elaborate display behaviour. They say water is essential for successful lovemaking. Lack of it never put my lotharios off the job – mallard are the gang-bangers of the avian world.

In their second year, ducks start to pair in late January, and the females go broody as the weather warms. One drake can cope with 8 ducks. All ducks will crossbreed, and often your pure-breed will fall for some free-flying wild Romeo mallard and subsequent ducklings may not favour their drake.

Place a couple of china eggs in the nest box to encourage the females. When a duck starts to sit and lines her nest with down, introduce any previously laid eggs you've been storing (somewhere cool and dark) or have brought in from a breeder. Remember: not too many. Too many ducks in your garden will result in chaos – do as I say, not as I did.

Place your broody duck with her eggs in a separate small house and make sure she has food, enough water to immerse and preen her head, and that mess is cleared daily. The incubation period is 28 days from the time she started to sit. When the ducklings hatch, they'll stay under mum for a couple of days, then she'll show them off – reward her with a big feed and clean out the nest.

Once hatched, keep the family in a separate covered run with a partially boarded top for shelter. Mum will call her babes over

ESSENTIAL VEG

There's nothing better than a plate of early new potatoes, dripping with butter and sprinkled with herbs.

- Chit a few earlies in a cardboard egg tray now, standing them blunt-end up.
- Leave them in a light cool place until they start to shoot.
- Place some crocks in the base of a bucket or similar container.
- Quarter fill with peat-free multi-purpose compost.
- Plant 3 spuds with their sprouts uppermost.
- Add a quarter more compost and keep adding more as shoots grow, until you reach the brim.
- Liquid feed fortnightly and water regularly.
- Harvest as soon as the foliage dies down.

to eat chick crumbs from your feed merchant served on a plate. Supply water in a small drinker so the ducklings don't jump in and get wet. Move the run every day to clean grass and open it at the end of a fortnight to let them out gradually. At this time, you can increase the size of drinker, too, but nothing too deep until they're fully feathered. Feed ad lib chick or turkey crumbs for the first 2 weeks, then growers' pellets and wet mixed corn. Ducklings can be sexed by late summer by their quack or croak.

Gardening with Ducks

Make sure you give your ducks plenty of space. If your entire garden is under cultivation, perhaps you can give them limited access for a couple of hours a day, or maybe during fallow autumn and winter months. Their two main downsides are the trample factor – ducks have big, flat feet – and the mess, especially round the pond, which can be cleaned with a burst from a high-speed hose. Vulnerable areas should be fenced off – they'll eat compost, and virtually anything green and sappy will be nibbled or trampled. Be warned.

Say goodbye to frogs, frogspawn and any other pond wildlife, too. You could install an extra pond with weldmesh panels over it to protect its inhabitants, if you like. Keep your duck pond ice-free in winter with a small electric heater, like those used by fish fanciers.

On the upside, your ducks will eat garden pests. Their droppings will fertilise the garden soil and their soiled bedding makes excellent compost when added to the heap layered with other garden waste. They get on well with other garden familiars, mixing well with hens. Your own cats and dogs can be trained to ignore them, but other people's pets can be a nuisance. Foxes are a problem, but worst are herons that fly in at dawn and spear the ducklings.

Keeping poultry encourages other birds into your garden – they'll use duck down to line their nests. I love to see the swallows gather mud from the pond's edges and swoop down to catch midges. Sadly, duck eggs and ducklings are on the menu to magpies, crows, jays and sparrowhawks as well as mink, squirrels, rats and stoats, which is why, in the wild, mallard have such huge families.

TIMELY ADVICE

Young hens will start to lay this month. Check the nest box daily.

Top up protein rations for all poultry.

Cut back cornus and salix shrubs; bring stems into the house or save for supports.

Lift and divide snowdrops after flowering.

Plant fragrant shrubs for next year.

Cut back autumn-fruiting raspberry canes to the ground.

Protect vulnerable fruit blossom from frost.

Possible Problems

Ducks are amazingly hardy creatures – mine survived with little input from me – but as with any kept animal, problems exist that you may encounter. Make sure they have plenty of space. If kept on the same bit of land for too long, worms will become a problem. Your vet will supply a remedy, but better to rotate their territory. Provide constant clean water to stop eye problems developing.

Rats are the poultry keeper's enemy number one. Deter them by keeping your feed in metal bins and make sure food is cleared away at night. Your house should be strong and built on concrete or raised on legs so rats won't lurk underneath.

All poultry develop breathing problems from damp bedding. Make sure yours sleep on dry straw, not hay that harbours moulds, and clean their house regularly. Offer access to shade, because sunstroke is not uncommon.

Smaller ducks and Muscovies will need one wing clipped to stop them straying. Watch your breeder do it the first time, and with luck your flock will have settled by the time the feathers grow and subsequent generations won't need it. Never trim feathers during the moult, however – ducks moult in September to November and your garden will be full of feathers.

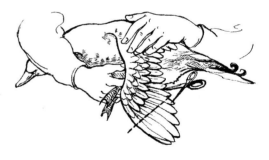

Catching ducks is difficult. A fishing landing net is useful in an emergency, but best to herd them gently into a cage. Always move slowly among your birds. Ducks are naturally friendly and inquisitive, but suspicious of wheelbarrows and hosepipes.

If you have to handle a bird, slide one hand under its tummy and grasp the legs, holding the neck under your arm (see illustration). Watch out for sharp claws, especially with Muscovies. If you need to transport them, pop them into a strong, ventilated cardboard box lined with newspaper and place on the back seat of the car, rather than in an airless boot.

If you need to cull a bird because of injury, take it straight to the vet. If you want to eat your surplus drakes, go on a course and learn how to kill painlessly, and pluck and draw effectively. Hopefully, your flock will live long and stress-free lives, giving you and your family lots of pleasure.

New-Laid Poached Duck Egg on a Bed of Spinach

A TASTE OF SPRING and a chance to eat your first homegrown meal of the year.

Stir a saucepan of simmering water to create a whirlpool.
Crack and drop in eggs one by one, waiting for the water to re-boil between eggs.
Poach each one for 3 minutes and remove with a slotted spoon. Leave to drain on kitchen paper.
Steam a panful of spinach and drain well.
Top a slice of hot buttered wholemeal toast with some of the spinach, create a nest and spoon in a poached egg.
Season with plenty of black pepper and sprinkle with snipped garlic chives.

Harden off your broad bean plants before planting out.

MARCH

POLLINATORS

Encouraging Pollinators
into Your Garden

Insect Pests

Eggstras: Quail

Lemon Curd

The sap is rising,

the days are starting to lengthen …

You'll feel the need to get out into the garden, so start clearing and weeding your beds and vegetable plots to get ready to sow. But watch out for late frosts, because March is nothing if not changeable.

Listen to the blackbirds' pinking songs as they argue over territory, to the fat bumblebees buzzing and braving the pale sunshine, watch the premature blossom flowering and shedding petals in the March gusts – these are the first and most eagerly awaited signs of life in the spring garden. It's these birds that will rid your garden of pests and these bees that will start to pollinate your plants.

People often worry that a wildlife-friendly plot is an untidy one. Not so: virtually any garden can be turned into a haven. By providing just three elements – water, food and shelter – you'll create a paradise where gardening without insecticides will bring major benefits to the creatures that have made their homes in your garden, without compromising your artistic dreams. We gardeners are pollinators' most important defenders, especially if we fill our gardens with nectar- and pollen-rich plants.

If we want to grow fruit and veg on any scale, we need pollinators to fertilise our plants to produce fruit and seeds. The past half-century has seen a decline in the number of bees and other beneficial insects that visit our plants, feeding on pollen and nectar, especially bumblebees (so useful to kick-start early fruit blossom), solitary bees, hoverflies, butterflies, moths and pollen beetles.

Keeping honeybees may be one answer to the problem of fruit germination, but encouraging insects generally is another option. For some time now I've felt uncomfortable keeping bees for honey and have decided to try and turn my garden into a haven for all pollinating insects.

Many beekeepers are becoming more bee-friendly: feeding their colonies on honey rather than sugar water or corn syrup; harvesting honey only once a year in spring, when there's an excess; disturbing them as little as possible and planting natural food sources nearby, rather than ferrying them by lorry to harvest crops miles away; and by building their communities from natural swarms rather than importing outsiders.

If you're already a beekeeper, consider keeping them in more natural ways: by using older hive designs, like the Abbé Warré one-size box hive, which uses comb rather than frames; in round Sun Hives made of woven straw and cow dung; and in top-bar horizontal hives that expose only small portions of the colony.

The Zeidler tree hive creates cavities inside living trees, making an attractive home for wild swarms of bees. There are also systems where you just turn a tap on the side of the hive, and honey flows out, and although this way boasts being less stressful to the bees, I worry that maybe it's the beekeepers' stress levels that are uppermost in mind.

Think about the insects themselves first, and create a beautiful buzzing arcadia in your garden that will benefit everyone – providing a comfortable habitat for all kinds of helpful bugs to keep your garden pollinated and productive.

Encouraging Pollinators into Your Garden

JUST A FEW SMALL CHANGES made now can bring more pollinators into your garden. By choosing the right plants, adding a pond and creating a year-round habitat, your plot could become part of a wider, interlinked local green space, and help stop the worldwide decline in these essential creatures.

Water

The single most effective way to bring all wildlife into your garden is to build a pond. Insects, mammals, amphibians and birds all need clean water. It doesn't have to be a beautifully designed water feature – a bucket or upturned dustbin lid in an out-of-the-way spot will do. Just make sure there's access via a gently sloping side or a small ramp so your drinkers can come and go as they please. Always supervise young children near ponds or cover the water with strong weldmesh panels. Insects, birds and amphibians will still appreciate them and plants can grow up through the netting.

POND POINTERS

Now is a great time to build a pond so it'll be ready in time for spring.

- Choose a site that's sunny but with some shade. If shade is provided by trees, net the area in autumn to stop leaves getting into the water, then decaying and raising nitrogen levels.
- If you have a water butt nearby, so much the better: you can rig up an overflow system with a hose, because rainwater is definitely best, and free.
- Try to build a pond with a deep area of about 50cm in the middle and a gently sloping shallow shoreline.
- Keep any subsoil to help smooth out the edges, then line your pond with sand, put down an underlay and cover with a liner.
- Neaten the edges with turf, rocks or wood to look as natural as possible.

Early bulbs in containers will encourage bees.

- Try to leave your pond plant-free and allow wild plants to grow. Many shop-bought non-native aquatic plants are a little too vigorous for small ponds, and several, including pennywort, water fern, water primrose and parrot's feather, have been banned because they grow too quickly and compete with indigenous water plants.
- During winter months, float a small rubber ball in the water to keep parts frost-free.
- Every spring, thin up to 25% of covering plants to stop overcrowding. Leave greenery on the side of the pond for a couple of days, so creatures can creep back into the water, and place the rest on your compost heap.
- Resist the temptation to put fish in your pond – they'll eat most insect larvae.

Habitat

Flowers receive a wide range of visitors, but not all insects are equally effective pollen depositors. Trials have proven that bumblebees, solitary bees and honey bees are the most successful, but hoverflies, wasps, beetles, midges, ants, spiders, butterflies and moths are also important to plants, moving between them collecting food and carrying pollen from one plant to another. So aim to encourage all sorts of insects into your garden by providing a mixed habitat.

WOOD PILES

Leave a pile of wood in a shady spot to decay, because dead and rotting wood and bark is a rarity in most gardens, but many beetle larvae (like the Devil's Coach Horse, which eats vine weevils) need this habitat, and it's valuable for fungi, mosses and lichens too. You can scatter logs in beds and borders as well, and make a home for a toad, where he can protect your plants from slugs and snails.

ROCK PILES

Piles of rocks, old clay roof tiles or broken flowerpots somewhere out of the sun make good locations all over the garden for beetles and slow-worms. Make sure you don't move the piles once built, so their inhabitants aren't disturbed. Song thrushes

Create shelter and grow early flowers to encourage pollinators.

will use the rocks as anvils to crack open snail shells, and amphibians will appreciate a rock pile near your pond, and will live under decking too.

BUG HOTELS

Make your own from a stacked pile of pallets, with their recesses and crevices stuffed with bundles of hollow stems, stacked tiles, pierced bricks, cardboard tubes, small sheaves of straw and terracotta flowerpots. Give the pile a waterproof roof and site it in full sun, facing south, because bees like to warm up in the morning. If you encourage long grass to grow round the base, the lower levels will be partly in shade for creatures that prefer a damp spot.

DEAD HEDGE

A barrier made of dead and decaying twigs, too big to compost, too small to burn, makes a desirable home and nest site for all sorts of creatures. The bottom of the pile will soon compost down, leaving a good habitat for beetles and small mammals. It can also provide a natural-looking barrier or windbreak around a pond or compost area. Plant several stakes along its length to keep branches in place and just keep piling new wood on top.

COMPOST HEAPS

Compost heaps should be part of everyone's gardening regime (see page 20), recycling garden waste into mulch, compost and soil conditioner. Your heaps will make a warm comfy home for wildlife, too – take care when dismantling during autumn. Recently, I put my hand into my builder's bag of leaves, and brought out a squirming handful of slow-worms. I popped them into the new bag very quickly.

MEADOWS

Meadows and beds where plants and grasses are left uncut during winter months leave lots of natural habitat for overwintering insects. You don't need rolling acres: a small patch of lawn in an open sunny position can be transformed into a mini-meadow, rich in insect-attracting wildflowers. I find the best way to introduce new flowers is to add small plug-grown

Make sure you grow year-round nectar- and pollen-producing plants for insects and their young.

plants in autumn. Try not to tidy away any of your garden plants until spring, leaving all your beds to die down. There's beauty in the natural decaying state.

NATURAL BOUNDARIES

A growing boundary hedge beats a fence or wall any day. Even better: make it a berry hedge packed full of fruit, nuts and seeds, like native hawthorn, blackthorn, crab apple, dogwood, hazel, spindle, bird cherry, elder or dog rose, with added ivy stems for shelter along with late summer flowers and winter berries. The base will still allow mammals to pass through your garden, linking it like a corridor to other green spaces.

Top Pollinators

Some insects are hard workers, and it's a good idea to encourage these by providing the living spaces they like best.

Mason bees like to nest in small rock piles, or 15cm-deep holes drilled in wood.

Leafcutter bees nest in holes in dead wood or old walls.

Hoverflies nest in compost heaps, where their larvae feed on rotting organic matter.

Solitary bees (240 species of wild bees that make individual nests for their larvae) nest in hollow stems or holes in wood in a warm sunny spot.

Lacewings and ladybirds will eat aphids and like to live in rolled corrugated cardboard or dry sticks stuffed into half a plastic bottle left open on its side.

Bumblebees will nest in an upturned flowerpot with access through a large drainage hole. Mine live in the ventilation bricks around the base of my house, and others make their nests in tussocky grass at the bottom of the garden.

Food

Food for pollinators – in the form of flowers, fruit and berries – needs to be available all year through. The result of a recent honey analysis in Westminster, London, showed that horse chestnut flowers were one of the bees' major feed stations. Trees

ESSENTIAL VEG

If you're short of space, like me, then grow multi-purpose vegetables, such as beetroot. You can enjoy their roots almost all year round, and also snip off their leaves to eat in salads.

- Sow your seeds now, in rows.
- Thin out the seedlings when they're big enough to handle.
- Water well and keep down weeds.
- Harvest every other beetroot when golf ball size, leaving the rest to grow bigger.
- Sow more seeds as soon as you have space.

are often forgotten on the list of bee-friendly plants. Obviously fruit trees are high on the list, especially apple, pear and cherry blossom, but lime trees and chestnut also provide thousands of easily accessible flowers, closely packed together. These keep flying miles down – bees apparently make separate journeys for different flower types. Single flowers offer easier access than multi-petal double blooms, too. Try to plant your insect-friendly plants in blocks, and remember night-scented flowers for moths, and caterpillar food plants like stinging nettles, bird's foot trefoil, broom, nasturtiums and wild grasses. Year-round insect food plants include:

Early: rosemary, aconite, snowdrops, crocus, hellebores, pussy willow, mahonia.

Spring: blossoms, chestnut, lime trees, currants, dandelions, pulmonaria, cyclamen.

Summer: lavender, helianthemum, cerinthe, clover, comfrey, alliums, honeysuckle, foxgloves, clover, knapweed, agrimony, guelder rose.

Late summer: verbena, echinacea, willowherb, buddleia, artichokes, thyme, achillea, mullein, artichokes, cardoons, leek flowers.

Autumn: sedum, blackberries, hebe, asters, origanum, abelia, caryopteris.

Winter: ivy, hellebores, winter honeysuckle, fatsia, arbutus, *Clematis cirrhosa*, sweet box, *Cornus mas*, winter-flowering cherries.

Insect Pests

NOT ALL INSECTS are the gardener's friend. Some are pests that need to be definitely discouraged. I grow lilies in pots. In the past, they've been decimated by red lily beetles, whose nasty larvae live surrounded by their faeces and strip the leaves. Last year I sprayed the stems, leaves and buds with a home-

made garlic spray and my lilies thrived. Luckily, the smell of garlic was overpowered by the scent of the lilies.

I mashed two or three garlic cloves in a mortar and pestle and steeped the mixture in half a litre of water. Mixed well, the liquid was left to macerate for a couple of days, then the bits were strained out and the liquid decanted into a spray bottle. I sprayed my lilies every day, from the moment they appeared through the soil, later avoiding the flowers and taking care not to spray near my face. I also made sure the bottle was kept out of reach of my grandchildren.

Some gardeners add a few drops of chilli oil or a squeeze of liquid soap to their sprays, both of which should be used with care. Garlic water and other home-made sprays can combat aphids, mites and whiteflies as well, but care should be taken not to deter beneficial insects at the same time with constant spraying.

Eggstras: Quail

INSECTS AND BEES are essential garden wildlife, but if you are keen on poultry (and don't have space for hens, ducks or geese) you can still offer a roost to endearing birds this springtime. With even the tiniest of gardens, there's still space for a few miniature egg layers. Why not try quails? With names like Bob Whites and Barred Buttons, and tiny babies like bumblebees, everything about them is charming. Their pretty bite-sized eggs are delicious hard-boiled and dipped in cumin salt, and some Japanese quail obligingly lay two a day in season. Encourage them with a ready-made nest of woven hay placed in a quiet dark corner of their tiny house.

Keep a small flock of 10 birds in a metre-square mobile run on the lawn in summer, or on the ground floor of an aviary, and they'll twitter engagingly as they bob up and down. Unable to climb ramps, they need a pop-hole at ground level. Feed your quail on pellets with added millet and budgie seed scattered on the ground to encourage foraging, plus plenty of clean water.

Lemon Curd

CURD IS A USEFUL TREAT to make with all those extra eggs as your poultry comes into lay. Sandwich it in cakes, ripple it through ice cream, eat it on hot buttered toast, and make meringues with the leftover egg whites.

Whisk together 2 whole eggs and 2 yolks in a jug.
Put 125g of cubed butter, 125g of caster sugar, plus the zest and juice of 2 lemons, into a heatproof bowl.
Pour in the eggs through a sieve.
Place the bowl over a pan of simmering water and cook, stirring continuously, until the curd thickens.
Spoon the curd into several small sterilised jam jars, seal, and leave to cool.
Store in the fridge, and eat within 2 weeks.
Use the extra whites to make meringues, and eat them sandwiched with lemon curd.

TIMELY ADVICE

Get your garden ready for spring, clearing away any debris to display flowers.

Deadhead bulbs and allow foliage to die back naturally.

Order your piglets and get sties and pens ready (see pages 167–169).

Prepare veg beds by manuring, weeding and mulching.

Stake, cover or cloche any vulnerable plants.

Keep an eye on straying hens, ducks and geese – they may be laying away.

Collect eggs every day to discourage your hens from getting broody.

Order fertile eggs from breeders if you want to hatch poultry (see page 77).

Protect apricot, peach and nectarine blossom with fleece, but remove on sunny days and encourage bumblebees to pollinate.

APRIL

HENS

Hens: Where to Begin

Rhubarb Vodka

Easter is such a
life-affirming
time of the year.

The days are lengthening, the air is sweet and I'm spending as much of my day outside as I can. I'm eating lunch in the garden as the sun warms up. Bunches of bulbs fill the house, fritillaries and bluebells are flowering in the meadow and woodland, and my seedlings are growing spindly on the windowsill. The blossom is falling like spring snow as I weed and start sowing spring salads and other leafy crops. The day's work done, I can toast the season with a glass of home-made rhubarb vodka, and best of all – the hens are laying.

I've been keeping a few hens in my garden for the past 25 years. I have no ambitions to supply eggs to Waitrose – just enough for me, plus extras to give away as presents. They're happy birds that supply me with delicious eggs, the garden is well-manured and flourishes, and my small flock of three bantam gold-laced Orpingtons gives me real pleasure as I watch them scratch about the beds, sunbathe and peck at plants. Obviously I don't want those plants to be ones I'd rather eat myself, so my birds spend time cooped in their run or out in the small orchard when I'm about.

My system is simple: buy 2 or 3 hens and keep them in a hen house sited inside a run, with as much access to your garden as their safety and your gardening ambitions allow. I plead the maximum free range possible for your hens, depending on how much you mind about your plants and their risk from predators – the more your birds range free, the healthier they'll be.

Set aside just 10 minutes a day and as much space as you can spare, and you'll reap rich rewards. Raising your hens naturally will be an eye-opener: they'll improve your garden's eco-system by eating garden leftovers and in return providing eggs for you, fertiliser for your plants and activating your compost heap.

Hens that lay for Britain, eat for Britain, and if what's on offer is your garden, then there'll be little left over for you, so I prefer to keep pure-breed hens rather than commercial hybrids that have been designed to lay an egg a day. By keeping these beautiful breeds, you'll help ensure their future and retain their valuable characteristics. Agricultural history will thank you.

Hens: Where to Begin

PICTURE A PRODUCTIVE GARDEN and you'll probably see a few hens pecking around.

They're easy to keep, and you'll be rewarded with baskets of eggs and cheerful companions. April is the perfect time to start your flock, and while keeping hens doesn't need to be complicated, it needs careful planning. First, check your house deeds or rental agreement to see if there are any contra-indications to your keeping hens. Next, and most importantly, check with your neighbours that they'll put up with any noise (not much if you're keeping just hens), and assure them that they won't be bothered with smells or vermin, because you'll be an exemplary poultry keeper. The promise of a few boxes of home-laid eggs might help too.

Next, decide where to site your run. Choose a place as sheltered, as spacious and as near to the house (so you can hear alarm calls) as you can – and if you've had a less than enthusiastic response from next door, as far from them as possible too. Your birds' main enemies are uncontrolled dogs, badgers, mink if you live near a river, and, of course, foxes.

Use your imagination when it comes to choosing a hen house (suppliers abound on the Internet); you could use an existing shed providing it's draughtproof, well-ventilated, waterproof and secure; or go for something bespoke that will fit your garden's overall style.

To help you decide which breed to buy, have a look on pages 74–75, where I describe my favourites. Finding your hens will be fun. Look locally first: ask poultry-keeping friends, visit a nearby feed merchant, and go to shows – you'll meet useful poultry contacts. Don't buy from auctions or markets: no one sends their best stock to market. Give yourself time, and always visit breeders' premises before buying from websites.

Finally, although keeping hens is easy, remember that you'll need to feed them twice a day – not easy in winter when suppertime is before dusk (hens go to bed at sunset), plus half an hour's poultry-maid duties once a week. But beware, it can develop into a consuming passion.

Where to Keep Your Hens

Hens are descended from forest-living birds, so the ideal site is a small, sheltered, sunny orchard or fenced woodland grove. My urban hens live in a 20 square metre run, fenced with bird-proof chicken wire 2 metres high, then reinforced with 1 metre high weldmesh panels around the base and camouflaged with climbing plants for extra shelter. I let them out of their run and into the main garden every day in the afternoon while I garden.

The bottom 15cm of netting are brought out into an apron and covered with paving slabs and turf to stop tunnelling predators. The ceiling is covered with loosely stretched woven fruit-cage netting, a cheap and easy way to stop foxes climbing on to the unstable roof of the run.

Within the run, out of the wind, sits the hen house. Painted in the same sandy yellow and slate grey as our house, it has a cedar-tiled roof and weather-boarded walls. So these pretty architectural details don't provide a home to parasites, the house is lined with thin plywood and all the joints are filled with mastic.

Short new grass is a great source of protein and greenery makes for yellow yolks.

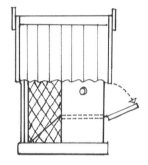

The house is on legs and the hens roost upstairs at night and underneath to shelter from the rain; it's easier for me to clean and make sure there are no unwelcome basement lodgers. I've boarded this area under the house to make a dust bath and filled it with wood-ash, adding a sprinkle of diatomaceous earth to discourage mites and lice. Sandpit sand or dry earth works just as well.

Inside the hen house, the floor is lined with newspaper so I can easily scoop the used bedding straight into the compost bin. I prefer chopped hemp bedding. Straw is often home to mites, wood shavings are hard to compost and hay is bad for birds because it harbours moulds. I fill the nest boxes with moss raked from my lawn to make them comfy. Change bedding weekly, and sprinkle sanitising powder every month or so. Once a year, completely blitz with a car Hoover or a really good sweep.

The floor of the run is covered with a good 15cm of hardwood chippings, fun for the hens to scratch about in, free from the mould spores in bark and perfect to stop the run becoming a mud bath in winter. If your flock spends its whole time in the

Buy, adapt or build a henhouse that keeps its occupants safe and sheltered, and that looks good, too.

run, the chippings should be changed bi-annually, and remember to give your flock access to grass in cut turfs or growbags sown with grass seed. Divide the run in half and use each side for six months at a time to prevent the build-up of worms in the soil, or buy a mobile run and house.

Choosing Your Hens

All domestic fowl originate from jungle fowl that range the tropical forests of Asia, but the variety of their descendants is amazing. You can choose from hundreds of breeds – from traditional backyard birds that are easy, amiable and widely available, to extraordinarily colourful, exotic and expensive fowl, probably not a good idea for beginners.

A cockerel isn't necessary for your hens to produce eggs, just to fertilise them, and you can buy fertile eggs from breeders if you want to hatch some. As a beginner I'd stick to hens, and let the amount of available space govern the size of your flock, not your enthusiasm or your appetite for eggs.

Most pure-breed hens lay very well in their first laying year (over 24 weeks); from March to November in their second and third years; and then their laying season decreases for the remaining 8 or so years of their lives. Some are better layers than others: the most productive ones need plenty of space and food. My recommendations below are for good garden breeds, birds that will happily range a garden without destroying it.

Pekin

Most breeds come in standard and bantam sizes. The smaller bantam hens have all the same characteristics as their larger counterparts. Their eggs are smaller, too – 2 hen to 3 bantam eggs in recipes. Big hens tend to be more docile and less noisy, while bantams are flightier and generally need less space, so are ideal for a really small garden.

There's also a range of commercial hybrids that lay an egg a day for 3 years. This laying burden effectively shortens their lives. They come in a range of egg-colour varieties and are usually mixtures of best laying pure-breeds. They make notoriously bad co-gardeners, because their laying is fuelled by a massive appetite.

Orpington

You could also give a home to ex-battery hens, designed to lay an egg a day for a year and then usually sent off for pet food. Not all survive the experience, but if you want the satisfaction of giving them a good home, make sure you don't mix them with other hens until they're quarantined, and keep them in a sheltered place until their feathers have grown back. Many go on to live happy lives, but if they don't, it won't be due to lack of care on your behalf.

Start with just 2 or 3 hens – you can always get a couple more in a year or two.

I try to hatch out a couple of hens every other year. This prolongs my egg supply, and every year I find a couple of my old ladies slip off the perch. Older hens make good mums and add stability to the flock.

PEKIN (CHINA)

A pretty bantam-sized bird with feathered legs that scratch less in the garden. Gentle, excellent sitters that need little space, and come in a wonderful range of colours and patterns. Highly recommended, especially for children. Lays small beige eggs.

Rhode Island Red

ORPINGTON (GB)
Large, docile and tame. A favourite of mine, which needs plenty of space. Lovely soft feathers available in buff, black-blue and white, and I recommend my bantam versions. Lays surprisingly small beige eggs.

RHODE ISLAND RED (US)
This traditional chocolate-brown hen lays lots of brownish eggs – up to 320 a year. A good forager, so not for sensitive gardeners, and long-lived, this utility bird is bright, alert and quiet.

SILKIE (ASIA)
A small breed that lays small beige eggs and is persistently broody on anyone's eggs. Available in various plain colours, with a funny little pom-pom on their head. Soft, with really silky hair-like feathers.

Silkie

SUSSEX (GB)
The classic Light Sussex has a black and white neck and tail, but also comes in buff, brown, speckled, silver and white. Good backyard fowl, laying tinted beige eggs, but needs plenty of space.

BRAHMA (INDIA)
Sedate and easy to handle: the gentle giant of the poultry world. Lays brown eggs and makes a good mum. Beautifully pencilled feathers that cover legs in light, dark, gold and buff Harris Tweed.

Sussex

What to Feed Your Hens
Hens are omnivores and need a basic diet of grain (mixed corn) and soya-based protein pellets which you will find for sale at feed merchants or pet food stores. When your flock free-ranges, these fundamentals are naturally supplemented by insects and greenery from the garden (short grass is high in protein). Nowadays, regulations prevent us feeding kitchen waste to poultry (unless you run a vegan household), and meat and fish are banned.

Water must be available at all times. Hens also need grit that they pick up from the soil to help them digest, and oyster shell

Brahma

for strong eggshells. Given access to a garden, birds are very efficient at balancing their own needs, but if confined to their run, you'll need to supply grit and oyster shell. Feed merchants and online poultry equipment sites sell everything your flock needs, and are a good source of information and advice too. Galvanised feed and drink containers are available, and also useful automatic feeders.

Chickens thrive on routine, so develop one that suits you all and stick to it. In the morning, I let mine into their run and feed them a breakfast of sunflower hearts and pellets and refresh their water. In the evening they get a handful of mixed corn. I give my hens a flowerpot saucer each to feed from and remove it when they've finished to discourage unwelcome diners.

Keep all your feed in a galvanised metal dustbin with a metal lid to deter rats and mice. Buy just a small amount of feed at a time so it's always fresh, and supplement with bunches of hanging garden greenery such as lettuce, cabbage or spinach leaves. Find out what treats your hens like by offering bits of garden-grown fruit, veg, nuts and seeds, and always clear away leftovers.

Moss makes a comfy nest-box liner.

Eggs & Chicks

If you order your birds in spring, they should be ready to collect in late summer, already laying if they are at point of lay (over 24 weeks old), and will carry on laying all year. In their second year, pure-breed hens normally lay from Valentine's Day to Guy Fawkes, though hybrids produce eggs throughout the year. I get a couple of eggs a day from my three 2-year-old bantams during spring and summer.

The egg is a perfect natural food: unrefined, unprocessed, unenriched, and free-range eggs really do taste best. The most versatile ingredient in your larder, they'll keep for 3 weeks in a cool spot, but the joy of owning hens is having everyday access to really fresh eggs. Depending on your breed, you'll get brown, tinted beige, white, speckled or even blue eggs. Clean

them as you collect with a piece of loofah or cloth. Don't soak them, because the shells are porous, and will lose their natural anti-bacterial bloom.

For a continuous supply of eggs, increase your flock by a couple of hens every other year. Hatching your own with a cockerel that runs with the flock is the natural way to build up stock, although nothing in nature is guaranteed. You can tell which eggs are fertile by candling them with a light from day 7 onwards (have a look on the Internet for good visual instructions). You can also buy fertile eggs of any variety from a breeder if you want to try a new breed or don't have a cockerel. The newcomers are introduced gradually as they grow, and can be released into the main run at 6 weeks.

To do this, you need an incubator (follow their instructions for use) or, better still, a broody hen. Any time during the laying season, you may notice a bird that wants to sit all day in the nest box, fluffed up and clucking, that pecks if you disturb her. If you don't want to hatch chicks, remove any eggs she's sitting on and shut her out of the nest box. It may take several days, but persist. Really persistent broodies will sit on any eggs: fertile or infertile, and will sometimes even sit without eggs.

If you want to hatch chicks, go back to the nest in the evening. Quietly move the broody hen to a small house or strong cardboard box lined with moss inside a separate run in a quiet place away from the rest of the flock. Carefully place any eggs you want to hatch under her.

Every day, at the same time, take her out and make sure she eats, drinks and performs her ablutions. She will protest. The incubation period lasts 21 days from the time she started to sit on the eggs. When the chicks hatch, they'll stay under mum for a couple of days. When they appear, offer them chick crumbs sprinkled on the ground and water in a saucer with an upturned flowerpot in the middle, so they don't get wet and chill. The mother hen will show them what to do: your role is supervisory.

This way of increasing your flock is best, but in nature, nothing is guaranteed, and you may end up with surplus cockerels that will have to be culled – a problem worth considering before you start. If you decide to keep a cockerel, he will be fine to breed from for one generation; after that you'll need new blood and to buy in fertile eggs.

Alternatively, chicks can be bought at 12 weeks old, but without a minder they will have to be raised in a separate run until they're fully grown and can hold their own.

You can also buy fully grown new hens at point of lay (20–24 weeks), but newcomers won't be welcomed by your existing flock. Whatever aged birds you bring in, keep them in a separate cage within the main run so the others get used to them slowly. Always buy in pairs so there's a familiar face. It can take a while for things to settle. There's always a pecking order in a flock, so make sure you don't keep too many hens, or the ones at the bottom will have a hard time. If a particular hen is doing the pecking, try cooping her and letting the victim run with the others.

An extra small mobile run made of 25 x 50mm battens, stained, screwed together and stapled with plastic netting, makes a useful refuge for new hens, a maternity ward or hospital, and when not in use protects your salad bed from unwelcome diners.

Gardening with Hens

Poultry make great pest controllers, first-class weed-seed eaters and land clearers, and over the years I've developed strategies to minimise the problems of gardening with hens so your garden and flock can flourish together. In winter, when the garden is fallow, your flock will provide the interest, movement and drama that's missing at this gloomy time of the year.

- Chicken manure can be used in three ways: first as a compost activator; secondly, when composted with layers of poultry bedding and feathers as a good soil conditioner or mulch; and finally, high in nitrogen and phosphates, it makes good fertiliser. Always leave manure to compost down first – used fresh, it will burn plants.
- Cover newly planted treasures instantly with a cloche or netting – it's the disturbed soil that hens find so attractive.

I let my bantams into the garden every day for supervised free ranging, to protect them from urban foxes.

You can place flints or pebbles round shrubs and trees to protect their roots from dust bathers.

- Vegetable plots are no-go areas, except in winter when they can be cleared and foraged by your flock. I used to keep my hens in their run during the green-to-go springtime period and they would all go broody. I've since decided it's easier to net my vegetable patch.
- A purpose-made dust bath under your raised house or like the one illustrated on page 72 should dispense with pockmarked beds.

Possible Problems

Most poultry problems are caused by stress, and birds made susceptible by overcrowding and trauma. Give them a peaceful life, plenty of space, good food, clean water and lots to amuse them and you'll be spared most of the textbook disasters.

If, however, one of your flock seems fluffed up, sitting and unwell, isolate her for a while (with food and water) and if she doesn't rally, take her to the vet. Vets that specialise in poultry used to be as rare as hens' teeth, but check the Internet – you may be lucky. Seek help immediately for an injured bird.

To catch a hen, best to take it from the house at night. Slide your hand under its breast and grab the feet, steadying the bird with your other hand on its back. Speak to her softly, and relax – stress is catching.

If your birds seem generally off-colour, dilute 20ml of cider vinegar in a litre of water in a plastic drinking container as a tonic, especially during the moult. All birds moult annually in late summer and they mooch about in various states of un-dress for about a month. The feathers will grow back through a transparent tube, which is then preened away. Never clip wings during the moult, as the growing feathers have a blood supply.

In very hot weather, make sure your hens have plenty of shade and the hen house is well ventilated and kept clean. If your hens are scratchy, it could be lice (small gold/grey insects with white eggs that stick to the base of feathers, especially around the vent). Dust your hens with diatomaceous earth powder.

If they seem restless and pale-wattled, with blood spots on their eggs, look for mites in the hen house – a more pernicious

TIMELY ADVICE

Keep weeds under control by hoeing mulches.

Continue to protect fruit blossom from late frosts overnight with fleece.

Pollinate apricot blossom with a paintbrush if there's a dearth of bees.

Rake moss from your lawn and dry it to line nest boxes.

Make sure indoor seedlings are turned, to stop them growing towards the light.

Sow annuals, veg and salads, but keep cloches to hand.

Transplant broad bean plants.

Keep harvesting leeks, asparagus, kale and rhubarb.

problem, especially during the summer. Check on a weekly basis at night with a torch and a piece of white paper: run it along the floor, and if it turns blood red, use diatomaceous earth on the birds, and thoroughly clean the house with whatever product is currently recommended for at least 3 weeks to block the mites' life-cycle.

If, for any reason, you have to cull a bird, it's best to call the vet or someone with experience. Probably you'll only ever have to do it once, not often enough to learn by practice. With a little luck, all your birds will live long, happy and productive lives, providing you with delicious eggs, cheerful companionship and enough enthusiasm to try again.

Rhubarb Vodka

RHUBARB IS THE FIRST FRUIT of the year, so make the most of it: eat it in fools, sauces and crumbles. Here's a way to toast the new season.

Take 5 or 6 red rhubarb stems, poach them in a little fresh orange juice and sweeten with sugar.

Pour into a wide-mouthed jar with a 950cl bottle of vodka – cheap will do.

Store in a cool, dark place for a week, shaking the jar every now and again.

Strain through a muslin cloth or sieve into a clean bottle. I'm not sure how long it keeps, because ours seems to disappear overnight.

MAY

HERBS

Herbs Through the Year

Washing Lines

G&T with Lemon Verbena
and Self-Heal Flowers

May is my
favourite summer month.

Full of promise, the garden has a sweet freshness, unsullied by the heat of high summer. The hens are happy eating protein-rich short grass and laying the beautiful yellow-yolked eggs that all that greenery triggers – only free-range hens with access to plants lay eggs of that particular golden hue.

My potted auriculas have been moved centre stage to a starring role in their theatre. This protects them from the sun and rain that damages delicate flowers and farina-floured leaves. Occasionally I briefly bring a particular beauty on to the kitchen table to admire for closer inspection.

The broad beans are flowering – I'm checking daily for blackfly – and I'm pinching out their tips and eating them raw in salads; the goosegogs are getting bigger – soon I'll thin them and take the thinnings to cook, leaving the others to fatten up as dessert fruit; and my first cut-and-come-again salads are cropping – I've picked some early as micro veg to decorate dishes.

In May I continue to sow salads in succession in small rows in the vegetable beds. My pea shoots are beginning to sprout and I like to start peppers and tomatoes in pots, to plant out into larger containers when they are big enough to handle. Courgettes and squash should be started now in pots and I plant pumpkins in my compost heaps, where they have plenty of space to race along the dead hedge behind them.

The blossom is nearly over, petals floating down like snow, and the trees in the orchard

now have a secondary role to the meadow, playing second fiddle to a riot of fuchsia-pink wild gladioli, royal-blue camassias and delicate waving grasses. These bulbs are the only non-native introductions to this area of wildlife-friendly flowers and grasses, though both grow prolifically in local gardens.

Fresh homegrown fruit and veg are packed full of flavour, but most are enhanced by the addition of a herb, both often reaching their peak simultaneously. Basil and tomato, carrot and coriander, gooseberry and elderflower, pea and mint, rhubarb and angelica: all are seasonal delights that grow together and go together.

Herbs Through the Year

EVERY HERB HAS ITS SEASON, from the hardy perennials like bay, rosemary, sage and thyme, whose gutsy flavours cheer up winter dishes, through spring-like shoots of mint, tarragon and sorrel, and summer's annuals, coriander, dill and basil, to autumnal chervil, fennel, savory and myrtle. Don't bother to dry herbs, they have a forgotten, dusty flavour – far better to use them at their fresh best.

Now is the best time to both enjoy and sow herbs, and you can grow them in pots, in containers, in beds and in rows in the veg plot. Use them in the kitchen to enliven your food, steep them in the bath to invigorate tired bones, strew them in the linen basket to make your washing smell lovely after a day on the line, and burn them in the hearth to sweeten the air. All are beautiful plants that enrich the borders with fragrant flowers and attract insects like sirens with their perfume and nectar.

In a small garden like mine, the plants I grow have to earn their keep. Herbs are multi-purpose powerhouses – legendary medicinal pharmacopeia – their petals, leaves, stalks and seeds will en your cooking, make you feel better and make your garden a richer place.

Spring Herbs

MINT – for the freshest taste in the garden

Grow in rich moist soil in a large pot, kept near a tap as a constant reminder to water. Greedy and fast-growing, it will overpower other herbs, so needs its own pot and can be grown in partial shade. Divide the roots occasionally and start again with new plants for fresh growth and to avoid mint rust. Spearmint is a useful variety.

Cook with new potatoes, broad beans and peas, or use fresh in a cucumber and yoghurt raita. It's surprisingly good with blackcurrants and melon, in an apple jelly, in a mojito, with chocolate or to flavour ice cream.

Bonus: high in antioxidants, peppermint oil is used in many remedies, especially for digestive problems. Mint tea is

Gooseberries taste good with elderflower and broad beans are delicious cooked with fresh mint.

particularly beneficial. Steep the bruised leaves in water, then use chilled as a facial wash.

TARRAGON – goes with almost everything

Grow in a deep container – it has long roots – and bring under cover as it dies down to protect it from winter cold. Tarragon likes gritty soil in a sunny site. Kept over winter in a greenhouse, tarragon will start to sprout early, offering its rich liquorice flavour as a spring bonus. Use chervil for a similar flavour later in the year.

Cook the young leaves sparingly with salmon, eggs, chicken, lamb, rabbit and in sauce béarnaise. I love it with a new-potato salad with soft-boiled eggs. Try it with fruit, or steep the leaves in white wine vinegar for a flavourful condiment.

Bonus: make tarragon butter and freeze for winter use, or wrap shoots round hard-boiled eggs, cover with cling film and refrigerate overnight before peeling.

SORREL – an astringent wake-up call to the system

Grow buckler-leaved sorrel with its arrow-shaped leaves for a pretty, tasty addition to any salad or sauce. I grow it in a row in the vegetable garden, where it seems to proliferate nearly all year, setting seed so I can give plants away to friends, or use the new plants to replace old ones.

Cook: I pick a handful of leaves to add raw to all my salads. With its lemony tang, without the sourness associated with other sorrels, it has the same surprising bite as capers or pickles. Sauté in butter and add pepper to make a sauce to drizzle in soups or over fish.

Bonus: use as a spring tonic, with an oxalic acid content similar to rhubarb. Try the seeds in salads too.

Summer Stars

CORIANDER – useful leaves, flowers, stems and roots

Grow in fertile soil in rows in the vegetable garden, in partial shade if you want leaves, or in sun for flowers and seed. Keep the compost damp to discourage bolting. To harvest seeds, cut stems and leave to dry in bunches.

Scatter rosemary, basil or sage flowers in salads to add a lighter version of the foliage flavours.

Cook as a base flavour in Asian dishes. Coriander brings out the taste of carrots and squash and enhances couscous, especially with a lime dressing. Try baking your own naan bread with fresh coriander. The seeds have a warm citrusy flavour and should be dry-fried, then crushed.

Bonus: coriander root is used in Thai curry pastes, whizzed up in a blender with garlic, chilli and herbs.

DILL – pretty, ferny annual with umbels that attract insects

Grow in a well-drained, sunny spot. The seed germinates quickly in the seedbed and needs thinning for strong plants. Cut fronds down to the base and the plant will regrow. Re-sow every month or so. Allow to flower if you want seeds.

Cook in all Scandi-style dishes, in dumplings, with smoked fish, with scrambled eggs on brioche, with yoghurt in a raita, with new potatoes and young beetroot. I love the fronds in salads, the flowers to decorate dishes and the seeds in vinegar pickles and salad dressings.

Bonus: try dill infused in vodka.

BASIL – the flavour of summer I can't live without

Grow under cover from seed in pots of rich, light, well-drained soil, then take outside into a sunny position. Pinch out tips to encourage bushiness, though the flowers are delicious as well. Keep sowing throughout summer to keep up with demand.

Cook with Mediterranean vegetables, especially delicious in basil, lemon and courgette soup. Try shredded basil with strawberries or white-fleshed peaches, and it's lovely in lime lemonade. Make pesto as the plants begin to deteriorate.

Bonus: keep a pot of basil in the kitchen to deter flying insects.

Autumn Flavours

CHERVIL – anise-flavoured ferny leaves, flowers and roots

Grow this biennial in damp part-shady soil and it will over-winter in a protected site. Harvest the leaves before it flowers, but leave one or two flowers to go to seed and you'll always find a few welcome plants popping up somewhere in your garden.

Cook by adding to dishes at the last minute, so as not to lose its delicate flavour. Chopped fine, fold into an omelette just before serving. Delicious with beetroot and asparagus or in a classic mayonnaise. Blitzed with a little olive oil, it makes a good drizzle for steamed leeks. Mix leaves with sea salt to make a dip for hard-boiled quail or bantam eggs.

Bonus: steep the leaves in hot water to make a refreshing tea that's supposed to cure hiccoughs.

FENNEL – seeds, stalks and fronds are all useful

Grow common fennel plants that can reach 2 metres high, and look lovely in the border or in a sunny meadow with good drainage, especially the bronze-leaved variety. The ferny foliage is better used young, and the flowers are a magnet to insects. Take care fennel doesn't seed itself everywhere.

Cook using the chopped fronds to stuff fish. Collect the seeds and add to buns and breads, pickles and soups, or make your own fennel salt.

Bonus: cut down the dried stems and use as fuel in barbecues for sardines and mackerel.

SAVORY – a compact perennial cousin to summer savory

Grow in a well-watered spot. It's easy to grow, so keep it compact with continuous snipping. May be a good companion plant to broad beans, as it is said to discourage aphids.

Cook with beans and as a salt alternative. I love its strong taste on grilled goat's cheese or to flavour cheese scones, and it's worth considering it in stuffings for turkey or chicken as a change from sage. In the past, Romans used savory instead of mint to flavour a vinegary sauce to go with lamb.

Bonus: grow savory near beehives for its flowers, to provide year-round nectar.

HERBS FOR SWEET DISHES

Lemon verbena – for an authentic taste of lemon.
Sweet cicely – adds sweetness to tart fruits.
Angelica – pop a stem or two in with your rhubarb.
Lavender – use parsimoniously to flavour puddings.
Tarragon – surprisingly, goes well with many fruits. Try it in apple tart.

Winter Stalwarts

BAY – one of my favourite smells in the garden

Grow in well-drained soil, in the garden or in containers. With shiny grey bark, the bay tree will grow to 12 metres if left unchecked. Easy to maintain, make sure plants don't dry out in summer or get checked by frost in winter. A cover of fleece might be appreciated in cooler spots. Prune in late spring with secateurs.

Cook by simmering in milk, then straining as a base for milk puddings, sauces and custards. Traditionally used to flavour bread sauce. Pop a few leaves in with your roast potatoes, and add to all hearty winter dishes, with lentils, with poached dried fruit. Delicious in a chocolate tart. One of the only herbs I'd dry, but since it's evergreen, fresh leaves can be picked all year.

Bonus: I have grown a bay hedge to separate my vegetable garden from the orchard. Some of the smaller-leaved varieties do well topiarised and all look good as standards. I dry leaves under a floor mat, bundle them up with a ribbon and pop them into Christmas cards, or oil them, then coat them with melted dark chocolate before peeling it off to decorate festive cakes and puddings.

ROSEMARY – flowers early, a gift to bees and cooks

Grow in poor, scrubby, well-drained soil from cuttings taken in late summer and autumn. Rosemary is evergreen and hardy – though not in northern frost pockets, where it does well in a portable container, moved under cover in winter.

Cook in dishes that need a lemony pine flavour. Steep sprigs in olive oil or good vinegar to use generally in the kitchen – it's good in most Mediterranean dishes. I love it in biscotti with orange peel and walnuts, and it also goes well with dark chocolate.

Bonus: burn prunings on an open fire – the oil-laden leaves will crackle and smell delicious.

ESSENTIAL VEG

Now that the danger of frost has passed, it's time to sow rows of salads every 2 or 3 weeks for continuous cut-and-come-again summer meals.

- Try chicory, chard, lettuce, radicchio, rocket and spinach.
- Make a shallow drill in your most friable well-drained soil and sprinkle on seeds.
- Keep watered and weeded.
- Snip off and harvest young. Each plant should give you 3 or 4 meals.
- Compost as they start to flower, then feed the soil and re-seed.

MYRTLE – a plant for all seasons

Grow by potting in gritty compost and place it near the house in winter for extra shelter and easy access during dark winter months. With fragrant, small, glossy bay-like leaves, blessed with fragrant cream flowers and furry golden stamens, pinkish stems and pretty blue/black berries, this plant has year-round appeal.

Cook in stews and soups, and with onions and pork sausages. With its warm spicy flavour, this is an ideal Christmas herb. Herb expert Jekka McVicar uses the berries to make myrtle rather than sloe gin.

Bonus: the leaves keep their colour and scent when dry, so use them to perfume linen and decorate the house at Christmas.

Washing Lines

ON BRIGHT, BREEZY DAYS, I dry my laundry on my newly erected washing line. Stretched between wooden poles is a rope that's hoisted with a cleft hazel pole, so fresh air gets to sheets and towels more effectively than the ubiquitous rotary drier. The downsides are bird droppings (however lucky) and shower dodging, but the rainwater acts as a fabric softener and the smell of fresh air as you climb into garden-dried bedding is well worth the effort.

Line-dry your clothes to save electricity, lessen greenhouse gas emissions, reduce wear and tear on your clothes and minimise static. Pegged properly – from the hem – clothes get less wrinkled and need less ironing (one of my least favourite and most neglected chores).

Like medieval washerwomen, you can also spread clothes to dry on top of fragrant bushes

and hedges, or select a bunch of aromatic leaves, like eucalyptus, juniper, cedar, and myrtle, then crush them fresh or soak them in distilled water to make an essence. Or you could sprinkle handfuls of leaves on rugs before vacuuming, or pop them into muslin bags to layer between laundry in drawers or in the airing cupboard. Most aromatic herbs will discourage moths.

G&T with Lemon Verbena and Self-Heal Flowers

A TANGY GLASSFUL to toast the coming summer.

Pour a couple of centimetres of gin into a long glass.
Fill three-quarters full with good tonic.
Add the juice of a whole lemon and 2 ice cubes.
Pop in a bruised lemon verbena leaf and a few self-heal flowers (prunella) – a member of the mint family found in lawns and traditionally used to heal wounds.
Stir and serve.

TIMELY ADVICE

Cover any new growth with cloches, nets or cages.

Take care to collect eggs: leaving them in the nest box encourages broodiness.

Plant alpine strawberries: *Fragaria vesca* 'White Soul' may escape the blackbirds.

Make sure your seedlings and young plants are watered and turned regularly.

Move tender plants out into the garden, but watch out for late frosts.

Clip evergreen hedges, hoe weeds and feed container-grown plants.

Stake all plants with pea sticks pruned from hazel and other garden shrubs.

JUNE

CUT FLOWERS

Decorating Your House

Gooseberry Water Ice with
Morello Cherry Sauce

Midsummer

and the living is easy.

Everything is in flower and I want to bring as many into the house as I can. They may be fleeting, and their beauty may be ephemeral, but memories of their smells last forever and take you straight back to childhood. Pity the poor child that only sniffs florist's blooms – they're usually odourless nowadays.

If I ever felt like showing off my garden, then June is the month I'd choose. Many years ago I started opening my previous garden annually for the National Gardens Scheme, and when I moved here, Kent NGS were keen to continue the tradition. I knew I couldn't muster the required 'forty-five minutes of interest', so I banded together with ten or so other gardens here, including our community garden and a guerrilla gardener, and we all opened together.

At the last minute, I always bitterly regret having agreed to participate, because the thought of being judged drives me into a frenzy of tidying to a level I'd normally never dream of, but on the day, exhausted and driven half mad with meticulousness, I throw open the doors and greet up to 500 visitors with a wan smile. And of course, I love it.

It's a great way to raise money for charity and fun to work with other gardeners. In future, we hope to encourage others to join us by bringing in school and almshouse gardens, and to get more Whitstable people to tidy their front gardens and show support for the NGS with a yellow balloon.

The rest of the month is spent lying fatigued on my old swing-seat, which I've surrounded

with potted lilies, dark red roses, sweet peas, lavender and other wonderful aromas, while the bantams peck idly around or plop down next to me. The friendliest one often joins me up on the seat, but doesn't enjoy the motion.

Dark red and magenta rose petals are the best for turning into jelly or crystallising with whisked egg white and caster sugar, applied with a paintbrush, then left to dry on grease-proof paper overnight. You can dry rose petals to use as confetti or decoration as well, by drying them separately on a mesh screen or baking rack until crisp – they'll deliver summer's smells into winter.

All around in the orchard and fruit cage, excess fruit is dropping from branches.

Fruit is naturally thinning itself. I pick my gooseberries and cook the thinnings, then leave the best ones on the branch to grow big and

fat and sweet, so they can be eaten straight from the bush. Keep an eye on all your fruit as it ripens, because your garden's wildlife will be waiting too, holding its breath for the moment it turns, and it will be gone. Use nets, cloches and cages to keep your fruit safe.

Decorating Your House

I AIM TO FILL MY HOUSE with something flowery all year round, or at least to pick a bunch of flowers for my kitchen table, keep something tiny that smells sweet next to my bed, a small posy for inspiration on my desk, and maybe a pot or two by the front door to welcome visitors and remind me of the season. It's not difficult, it just takes a little planning and imagination to have flowers, greenery and pots flowering every month to cut and take into your home. So, while most of your plants are looking after themselves, take time to look over your flowering agenda, so there'll be something to bring into the house every month.

January

It may be gloomy outside in January, but fill your house with indoor bulbs – sweet-smelling narcissi and hyacinths, and exotic orchids and amaryllis – and you could be holidaying in the tropics. Every year in summer, the bulb catalogues come plopping through the letter box, and a little thought now will result in lovely bowls of flowers and pots of bulbs during the dark months. Plant in pretty pots and cover the soil with pebbles or moss (scarify your lawn, there'll be plenty in shady areas).

Planted in bulb fibre in a bucket in October and left outside somewhere dark, bring *Narcissus* 'Cheerfulness' gradually into the warm once the shoots are about 10cm tall. *Narcissus* 'Paperwhite' can be planted in water with stones in a glass jar or pot. Fill up the pot with water just under the bulbs and place in a cool dark place until they shoot and produce roots. Move to a sunny windowsill but make sure they don't dry out.

Grow hyacinths in pots of well-drained compost with their shoulders showing. Water after planting and place somewhere cool and dry until green shoots appear, then bring in to a warm sunny spot. Only water if the soil is completely dried out, because these bulbs are prone to rot.

Amaryllis arrive ready to pot, so keep them in a cool, dry and dark spot until 6–8 weeks before you want them to flower, then pop them into a small pot with just an inch extra round the bulb in very well-drained compost. Place in a cool dark room for 2–3 weeks, then bring the buds into the light, but not into direct sunlight. Support the flower heads with pretty garden twigs that are just beginning to leaf.

Cymbidium orchids are easy to grow. I have several bucketfuls that spend their summer in the garden, and come the frosts, they're moved on to a light windowsill in the bathroom. I water, feed and stake the flowering stems, and as they flower, I bring them centre stage. The blooms last a long time.

February

This month needs flowers to cheer us all up, and if you look carefully, there will be a wealth of tiny shoots outside. Perhaps you want to give a loved one (or yourself) something special on Valentine's Day? Then eschew the garage or supermarket and pick something special from the garden. It's surprising what's out there flowering, trying to catch the early bumblebee.

Choose an interesting vase, but don't limit yourself to traditional ones. I'm a great car boot fair forager, and go out most

HOW TO LOOK AFTER CUT FLOWERS

Pick all your flowers in the early morning.

Pop them immediately into a bucket of cold water.

Strip all the leaves that would otherwise go under water, to prevent rotting.

Re-cut all the stems cleanly at an angle with a sharp knife or scissors.

Leave your bucket of blooms in fresh water in a cool dark place to recover for at least a couple of hours.

Sear droopy stems in just-boiled water for 20–30 seconds.

Arrange your blooms in a vase with 1 tablespoon of vinegar per litre of water.

Keep your arrangement out of the sun and away from radiators.

Change the water every other day.

Sundays to search out containers, from industrial metal tins and boxes to toys and cooking utensils. Most can be spray-painted or cleaned to spruce them up or they can be left as they are for a weathered look. Fill the container with scrunched-up chicken wire to keep your stems in place.

Flowering cherries will be blossoming, sweet box (*Sarcococca confusa*) covered in fragrant ivory flowers, ferny-leaved *Clematis cirrhosa* nodding with pale cream spotted bells, daphnes, hellebores, mahonia, witch hazel and winter jasmine all secretly doing their thing.

Give your arrangement structure with pussy willow, hazel or birch twigs, or pick interesting overwintered stems of perennials. Add texture with foliage: try *Arum italicum* 'Pictum' or any of the euphorbias, and for scent, pick any of the winter herbs – rosemary will already be in flower.

March

By now spring will have sprung and fruit trees will be beginning to shoot. I bring in branches of pear prunings, just before the buds are about to burst, and the warmth of the house brings them into leaf and bud. In March my cherry plum, with its coppery-coloured leaves and pale pink blossom, has been flowering since January, and my wall-hugging flowering quince – chaenomeles – are full of creamy or terracotta flowers. Some shrubs like buddleia, ceanothus, the dogwoods and hebes actually like to be pruned back at this time of the year, and many will grow roots in water so you can plant them out later.

Look around: forsythia, flowering currants, *Cornus mas*, escallonia, viburnum are all blooming and even berberis has golden racemes. Imagine a huge bucket of camellias or magnolias. Show off your branches in a large container and give them plenty of support, adding a large rock or pebble in the base to keep the arrangement stable.

April

By this time of the year, I'm a bit mean about picking from the garden because I'm spending more time out there and enjoying blooms in situ. So a series of little bottles (collected from my

ESSENTIAL VEG

Freshly picked peas are a delicious dish with homegrown mint, and you can eat the shoots very soon after they've sprouted.

- Plant peas in rows now, in a sunny weed-free spot in moist, well-manured soil.
- Stake the plants with hazel twigs and water well as flowers start to appear.
- Protect from pigeons with a netted cloche or tunnel.
- For pea shoots, sow thickly in a drill in fertile soil.
- Harvest when not too large and sweet, and leave roots in the ground to enrich the soil.
- Water well and keep weed-free.
- Harvest as soon as they're easy to handle, snip and serve.

grandsons' favourite fruit juice tipple) are perfect to showcase what's flowering in profusion outside. Bunch the bottles together in a crate, line them up in rows, or display collections of a particular flower – a row of different tulips is especially lovely. It's a charming way to bring the garden inside.

With even the tiniest garden, we shouldn't begrudge one example each of our favourites. I love showing off my *Narcissus* 'Thalia', *Narcissus* 'Pheasant's Eye' and muscari, plus wood anemones and bluebells from the woodland garden with fat pussy willows – there are white ones (*Salix alba*), yellow ones (*Salix hastata*) and even black ones (*Salix gracilistyla* 'Melanostachys').

May

I'm slightly potty about auriculas. They're one of those heart-stopping flowers that defines the season and they flower now: their little faces, their personalities and their palette of jewel colours, from emerald to jade, ruby to amethyst, silver and gold, pearl and jet, bring out the miser in me.

I display my plants in a home-made theatre (a car boot set of shelves) with a dark painted background, and occasionally bring them into the house on a windowsill out of direct sunlight so I can gloat over them in comfort. I particularly adore the ones with green-edged flowers and farinaceous leaves like 'Beechen Green' and 'Prague', but there are hundreds of colourways to collect. I also love the relationship between the auricula's floury-coated leaves, the muted flowers and the weathering on an ancient terracotta pot – one of the most romantic partnerships in floristry.

Available from specialist nurseries, these precious plants need protection from rain in winter and from the sun in high summer. Pot them in two parts John Innes No. 2 and one part horticultural grit in 10cm pots. Cover the surface of the soil with grit and feed these lovelies in spring.

June

Sweet peas are everyone's favourite June flower. I plant mine in October in root trainers and they spend their winter behind the house by a sheltered wall. They come out into the garden in

April, into fertile moisture-retentive soil, and climb their way up the chicken run's wire. Water your plants well, pinch out the leading shoots, nipping their stems just above a set of leaves to develop strong plants, and pick each flower as it blooms. The more you pick, the more you'll get.

Think of sweet peas and you think ruffles of pastel hues, but I love the darker ones: the purples, like 'Dark Passion', the maroons ('Cupani' and 'Almost Black') and the magentas. Scent is essential, so all the modern scentless varieties are out – I usually plump for Spencers. Pick them for as long as they last, discouraging seed setting and filling the house with their honeyed scent.

July

My south-facing front garden is a mass of lavender plants, at their headiest now. I chose *Lavandula* 'Grosso', an *officinalis/latifolia* hybrid, because of its intense fragrance, compact shape and dark blue flowers, and added lots of grit to the site.

Every September, after the bees have finished with the myriad flowers, I clip off the stems and collect them to put in a big rectangular basket in the scullery, and it keeps its perfume well until the following year. A bunch tied with a ribbon sits on my pile of drying-up cloths in the kitchen, but lavender has a multitude of uses from medicinal to culinary.

Lavender flowers attract hoards of pollinators, make lovely confetti, can be used sparingly to flavour sugar for tisanes, are delicious added to a basic shortbread biscuit dough and are even relaxing popped into a hot bath.

August

Succulents are my other horticultural guilty secret, and they are at their best in August. I've been quietly collecting them for years, and suddenly they've become a popular hipster plant. It helps that they are really easy to grow, but both tender glasshouse and hardy garden varieties are strangely addictive – for me, any visit to a nursery is incomplete without a new one to add to my collection. And there are thousands to choose from.

Apart from groaning shelves of tender echeverias, agaves and crassulas sheltering in my porch, I grow a patchwork of hardier

Collections of plants always look good together. Keep your passions well displayed, so others can admire them too.

sempervivums and sedums in gravel beds like Persian carpets to either side of my front door. Some pots in their prime spend time on the kitchen table.

Crassulaceae are accommodating plants, thriving on benign neglect and easy to propagate by picking offsets – leave them for a couple of days to callous over, then push into a pot of very gritty soil. With flowers like riotous fireworks, these plants look fab in unusual containers – mine thrive in lead, galvanised metal and terracotta pans in a mix of John Innes No. 2 and grit.

September

Autumn is creeping nearer, and it's time to forage the hedgerows for berries to display. Even a huge bucket of brambles can look stunning. Add a few sloe branches and some rosehips and you have the season on tap. All woody stems should be cut at a 45° angle with an additional vertical cut of 5cm through the stem, then seared for 30 seconds in water that has just boiled.

Plants with distinctive berries include mahonia's navy blue, elder's nearly black, sea buckthorn's pale orange, callicarpa's bright purple and spindle's bright pink four-part capsules. All the crab apples look wonderful in branchfuls, as do amelanchier and the not so desirable and rather rampant pokeweed berries. All berried plants will attract wildlife to your garden – both mammals and birds need these fruits, so leave plenty to keep them going through the winter months.

October

I know a few pumpkins like 'Marina di Chioggia' and 'Muscade de Provence' really do taste good, but I'm not a fan, so I grow mine for their decorative value: long fat 'Jumbo Pink Bananas', green and yellow ribbed sweet 'Tonda Padana', and beautiful blue/grey 'Baby Blues'. 'Rouge Vif d'Étampes' is a jolly bright crimson, 'Crown Prince' a stylish bluish-grey, and white varieties like 'Lumina', 'Polar' and 'Cotton Candy' add an eerie albino glow.

Piled high in my porch and festooned with Virginia creeper, they give a natural Hallowe'en feeling to a time of the year that has been hijacked by transatlantic tat. I've seen pumpkins carved with wood grain, covered with glitter and bejewelled with

TIMELY ADVICE

Cloche and cover fruit, especially strawberries.

Sniff as many roses as you can – on the street and in other people's gardens.

Remember to cut back your cow parsley before it sets seed.

Pick elderflowers to make cordial and freeze in small plastic bottles.

Pick lime flowers to dry and keep in an airtight jar for tisanes.

Make sure your poultry and pigs have shady places to escape the sun.

Keep on top of the weeding – a gentle hoe will dispatch most weed seedlings.

Plant out any veg plantlets as their roots reach the base of the pot.

thumbtacks, but nothing beats their iconic shapes and autumnal colours. Try growing gourds over an arch, and when their leaves disappear at first frost, the gourds hang on and naturally decorate your garden's entrance.

November

November is the month to squirrel away autumn's most colourful leaves, placing them between sheets of newspaper under a mat or runner. Special finds include heart-shaped cercis leaves in various shades of ruby red to orange; buttery-yellow winged ginkgo and felty white poplar leaves, as well as all the acers, sorbus, *Parrotia persica* and the spindle tree's rich orangey red foliage.

I also collect seed heads and flowers to dry for festive decorations. Most can just be hung upside down in bunches somewhere dry. I pick cardoons, physalis lanterns, papery honesty and nigella seed heads, and dried blue pom-pom echinops and spiky sea holly flowers. Allium and leek heads are spectacular, especially *Allium schubertii*.

Then, they are all waiting in the wings until their time comes to star, either sprayed copper, silver, gold or ghostly white, or left naturally beautiful.

December

Christmas is the time to show off all your growing and decorating skills, to turn the produce of your garden into unique decorations and create tiny ephemeral works of art that will embellish your celebrations with style and grace.

Turn cardoon heads and little pumpkins into nightlight holders (with patience and a sharp knife); string seed heads and dried flowers on to garlands and into tree decorations; and make wreaths and window surrounds from branches, twigs and climbers.

Stick dried leaves on to windowpanes and catch the light through them, glue-gun them on to wire wreaths or make them into lanterns, and watch candles flicker. Celebrate Christmas and bring the winter garden into your home.

Gooseberry Water Ice with Morello Cherry Sauce

A LUXURIOUS PUD straight from the garden.

Poach your goosegogs in a little elderflower cordial until soft.
Add extra sugar if you need it.
Strain if you don't like the pips – I love the extra crunch.
Place in a shallow tray and freeze.
Take out and break up the crystals with a fork.
Re-freeze, then eat with a sauce made of morello cherries
    cooked with sugar to taste, then strained and cooled.

JULY

BERRIES & CHERRIES

Berries

Escargots?

Broad Bean Houmous

Nothing is nicer than patrolling the garden on a July morning.

I walk through the trees and bushes after feeding the chickens, looking for newly ripened berries for my breakfast. Even better, to do it again later with my grandsons, searching for tiny alpine strawberries hiding in among their pretty palmate leaves, and popping them into berry-stained mouths.

Fruit is easy to grow, rewarding to pick and attractive to all your garden's occupants. One of the major hurdles to getting a reasonable harvest is competition from the birds, so make sure you get your fair share. The art of defensive gardening teaches lessons about watchfulness – patrolling your beds and orchards, checking often to see how ripe your fruit is, then netting, caging and covering your bounty in a way that's safe and secure – for both wildlife and fruit.

There are net tunnels that will protect strawberries and still allow the air to circulate; special cherry branch covers, cloches and cages, but the simplest deterrent to get full value from your berry bushes is to invest in a fruit cage, even a temporary one made from netting and stakes, or to grow fruit against a wall and peg on a protective cover.

Like little bonbons, packed full of sweetness and vitamins, many berries are rarely grown commercially, so often the only way to sample them is to grow them yourself. And all taste best straight from the bush. They lose most of their flavour in transit on the long journey from grower to seller, and while some are spoiled by cooking, others taste best foraged from local hedgerows.

Any fruit that's slightly damaged can be given as treats to pigs or poultry. Nothing makes for friendlier stock than little extras, but don't overdo it or they'll be too full up to eat their feed. Red is a colour that's particularly attractive to birds, and they'll all be waiting for that arresting colour change. Try growing white strawberries or currants or pale cherries to see if you can outwit them.

At this time of the year, it's possible to feed yourself from even the smallest plot. With a few eggs, small helpings of berries, daily pickings of salad leaves and herbs, some waxy new potatoes, your garden is a larder for the simplest meals straight from plot to plate. This is the real good life.

During the summer, I'm torn between my beach hut and my garden in the long summer evenings. Nothing beats a Whitstable sunset seen from the beach, but I miss the cool green calm of an orchard evening, sitting with my garden familiars waiting for dusk to fall.

Berries

GROWING BERRIES IS ONE of the most rewarding pursuits of all. Pretty, easy and sweet, all they need is a little care and a watchful eye, and you can enjoy fruits from spring through to autumn. Why not try a few of the more unusual varieties when you are planting later in the year?

While your berries are bearing fruit, remember to patrol your fruit beds every day, gently squeezing, sniffing and watching. Obviously the vagaries of the weather will affect exact harvest dates, but you can expect forced rhubarb in March and April, honeyberries in May, and gooseberries and redcurrants in June. July brings black and white currants, and cherries; August blackberries, September elderberries and autumn raspberries, with pointilla berries in October. All the berry shrubs like a well-drained, moist, fertile soil.

Gooseberries

These furry berries make good standards and can be easily grown in containers. They will also grow in partial shade under trees. Once a popular fruit with many special local varieties and clubs trumpeting their particular glories, the goosegog is no longer a common commercial fruit, and the future of many ancient types is probably now in the hands of gardeners like us.

Try to find an old variety local to you, or try 'Rokula', a new early red, 'Early Sulphur', a mid-season yellow, and 'Invicta', a vigorous bush with large green berries. All should be thinned in May by almost half their crop. These thinnings can be cooked with plenty of sugar, leaving space for the others to grow to full dessert size that can be eaten straight from the bush.

Prune your bushes in winter to remove dead, crossing and diseased wood. Then prune all side-shoots to 2 buds from their base. In July shorten all non-fruiting stems to 5 leaves. Try to leave the centre of the bush free of branches, to discourage mildew.

Gooseberries have a particular affinity with elderflower cordial: try it as a sweetener, and turn your harvest into compotes, jams and fools. They should be topped and tailed with scissors before cooking. They can be cooked whole, then strained, but

you'll lose the crunchy seeds that are such a special part of a gooseberry fool. Try gooseberry sauce sandwiched with sweetened mascarpone in a Victoria sponge, or in a sorbet or water ice with a morello cherry sauce (see page 115).

Alpine Strawberries

Fragaria vesca tolerates shade, and fruits little and often from May to October (known in the trade as 'everbearing'). Neat little plants to edge a bed, but be careful, some varieties can take over if you don't remove some of their many creeping suckers, though these would make good ground cover.

They're not as large or as juicy as their cultivated cousins, but their flavour is essence of strawberry – musky with vanilla and slightly acidic – and you'll only need a few to flavour a bowl. Sprinkle them with a little sugar and leave them for a while to let the flavours really come out. Wild strawberries make the most amazing jam, but you'd need at least 50 plants to make a single pot.

Make sure you patrol your crops everyday and pick as soon as they're ripe, or you'll lose them to other beady-eyed diners.

'Alexandria' is the easiest variety to grow. I grow the white ones too – *Fragaria* 'Tubby White', 'Pineapple Crush' and 'Leo White', to fox the birds. It really works – they ripen unnoticed, but you have to check regularly if they're softening or you'll miss them too.

Honeyberries

Also known as firstberries and mayberries – honeyberries (*Lonicera caerulea* var. *edulis*) are natives of chillier climes (Siberia, northern China and Japan). They're a great alternative for those who can't grow blueberries because they don't mind alkaline soil. Plant in pairs for good cross-pollination, in a sunny spot, to enjoy early berries in late May and early June. They'll turn blue and then bloomy with purple flesh when ripe.

Pretty plants with blue/grey foliage, they are well worth growing in the flower garden, where the birds may not expect them and may leave them alone. The Japanese varieties ('Blue Moon' and 'Blue Velvet') are the tastiest, a sort of sour and sweet taste, like a blueberry/blackcurrant mix. In the USA, where honeyberries are commonly grown, they are eaten in pies, pancakes and smoothies.

Morello Cherries

These sour cherries can be grown fan-trained against a north wall. A useful small tree for an unloved spot, it will produce cherries perfect for cooking and best for cherry jam. The cherries don't keep well, so make sure you're ready to get jamming as soon as they ripen. Earliest to flower among the fruit blossoms, give your bumblebees a good life, treat them well and they'll reward you by pollinating early. If not, these trees may need you to help by transferring pollen with an artist's paintbrush.

Prune branches back in late summer after harvest to 2 side buds from the main branch, to keep the tree flat against the wall. Never prune in winter or you'll encourage disease. Morellos are self-fertile and make good pollinators for other cherry trees. They're thirsty trees, but do badly on a waterlogged site.

Serve these dark red beauties poached, with a dark chocolate sauce reminiscent of a Black Forest gâteau, or try them stirred into thick Greek yoghurt with honey to sweeten. Sour cherries are also traditionally cooked with duck.

Jostaberries

These are a cross between gooseberries and blackcurrants, with black berries slightly larger than their blackcurrant parent. Thankfully, they haven't inherited the goosegog's prickles. Propagated easily from 25cm cuttings poked straight into the soil; I've planted them in a long thin bed against an east-facing wall, where they grow to about 2 metres tall. I've also grown them successfully as standard lollipops. They seem resistant to most berry problems.

When ripe and black, the berries taste like blackcurrants with a gooseberry bite. I share mine with my garden's blackbirds, but I have so many, I don't mind. I pick a few every morning from late July to the end of August to go on my muesli, and try to make at least one jar of really excellent fridge jam by mashing a bowl of berries with a little sugar to taste, then simmering for 5 minutes. It keeps in a jar in the fridge for a week or so, but is very popular, so doesn't need to last any longer.

Blackberries

Blackberries grow wild in hedgerows. There are hundreds of varieties, ripening from July until October, but after the first frost they are said to have been spat on by the devil – in fact there's little as unappetising as blackberries past their prime. Choose plump, shiny tender berries grown away from roadsides – they're best not washed or they'll disintegrate. Purée and sieve to make a coulis, or cook with apples in a classic autumn crumble.

Cultivated blackberries are more productive, but lack the frisson that free foraged fruit gives. You can train them against fences, and keep them under control by tying in new canes and cutting back all side-shoots. I suggest 'Oregon Thornless', otherwise you'll be pinned down by prickly wands.

Autumn Raspberries

'Primocanes' flower and fruit on the current season's growth, so you can prune them by simply cutting back all the canes to ground level in February. Train on wires attached to posts 60cm apart, running from north to south, or on individual bamboo canes in a sheltered spot. They will even survive unsupported.

The summer fruiting raspberry is ready at the same time as lots of other berries, so it makes sense to grow the autumn one, and by the time it fruits, its main enemy, the raspberry beetle (which populates berries with tiny white maggots), has disappeared too. 'Autumn Bliss' is a good variety that is harvested up until October, and 'Allgold' has yellow fruits.

Try popping a few late berries into white wine vinegar to make a condiment that goes well with beetroot; sprinkle them on breakfast muesli with oat flakes and flaked almonds; and freeze them separately as hot weather mini ice-lolly snacks for children.

ESSENTIAL VEG

I grow leeks throughout the year. They're delicious and much easier to grow than onions. Even the flowers are pretty and a magnet to bees. Save seed now.

- Sow seeds sparingly in drills throughout the growing season.
- Space them out when they're about 15cm high, lifting them carefully.
- Water them in, puddling them in good soil.
- Harvest when about 2.5cm in diameter.

Elderberries

Sambucus canadensis and *S. nigra* are often overlooked, despite their presence in every hedgerow. They're definitely better eaten cooked than raw and add a richness to other autumn fruits. Strip them from their stems with a fork and turn them into syrup, or steep them in vodka with a twist of lemon peel for a Christmas tipple.

Packed with anti-inflammatory and anti-viral antioxidants, these berries are a good source of vitamins A and C, iron and potassium – no wonder my bantams eat them with such gusto. Grow elderberry bushes in the orchard and you'll have flowers to make cordial in early summer and berries late in the season.

The more handsome dark-leaved pink-flowered elderberry bushes, like 'Black Beauty', have edible berries too, but the red-berried *Sambucus racemosa* is poisonous.

The Autumn Olive

Elaeagnus umbellata ripens from October to November. With delicate silver olive-tree-like leaves, this is a new fruit from Swiss fruit company Lubera, sold under the name 'Pointilla'. You'll need two bushes (they're not self-fertile), a yellow and a red one, and they will berry up prettily from August onwards, but take a while to ripen.

Jumping the gun, I've tried pointilla berries many times and been disappointed, but left until November, they taste good. Elaeagnus are very ornamental and could make a useful small hedge, and while the yellow berries taste a little watery, the red pack a punch, so they complement each other and make a good pair, both on the bush and on the plate.

Escargots?

THIS MAY BE A TACTLESS SUGGESTION, especially if, like me, you're putting out dishes of beer every evening to catch molluscs, but have you considered raising edible snails? The ultimate slow food, snails have been part of our diet since Roman times, and are a cheap source of protein and minerals – and July is the perfect month to buy and raise your own.

Helix aspera do well in our mild damp English climate (you're telling me), but these are bigger and faster-growing than their cousins, the common garden snail. In summer they must be protected from predators, especially the ones you've been encouraging for quite the same reason, like birds, shrews and hedgehogs; and in winter, snails hibernate.

Hatched eggs are available and you can grow them in your vegetable garden, feeding on anything that grows, for 3–6 months until the edge of their shell turns up like the brim of a hat – at which point they're ready for a long slow cook in a well-flavoured stock. Have you tried snails with bone marrow on toast or with mushrooms and truffle oil? They have a meaty texture and a delicate earthy taste. I promise.

TIMELY ADVICE

Make sure your hen house and piggery are adequately ventilated during heatwaves.

Replace doors with weldmesh panels to create a cooling draught.

Clean out houses and refill drinkers more frequently during hot spells.

Watch out for sawfly caterpillars on gooseberry bushes – another snack for hens.

Summer prune your gooseberry branches that haven't fruited.

Water crops and container plants early in the morning or in the evening.

Summer prune cordoned apples and pears.

Broad Bean Houmous

A QUICK AND EASY summer dip that's delicious with pitta or
sourdough bread.

Put a couple of handfuls of cooked broad beans into a blender.
Add an avocado, a sprig of fresh mint and the juice and zest of
  half a lemon.
Whizz together and season.
Drizzle with olive oil, decorate with mint leaves and serve
  straight away.

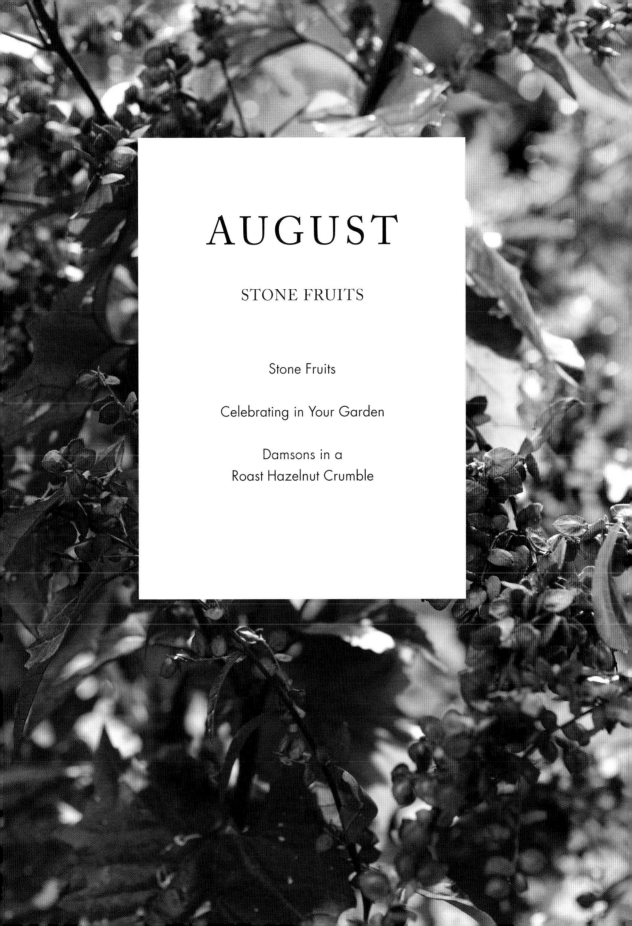

AUGUST

STONE FRUITS

Stone Fruits

Celebrating in Your Garden

Damsons in a
Roast Hazelnut Crumble

There's an art

to relaxing in a garden

you care for.

How do you switch off and ignore that wilting plant, that blinding clash of colours or unfortunate partnership, allow your mind to drift, and take pleasure in an environment where you usually labour? This is the gardener's dilemma in August.

Try to find an area with a view of the sky and horizon, a few swaying branches, some waving grasses to hypnotise you into serenity. Let your mind wander down avenues other than the garden path. Make sure you're comfortable. Most garden furniture is functional and needs mountains of cushions to soften the hard edges. Then close your eyes and try to stop your thoughts meandering back to the garden . . .

For just a few hours, forget the fact that the container plants need watering; that the hen house should be cleaned more frequently in warmer weather; that the salads are bolting and the early apples should be picked before they drop and damage. Dream instead of all the delicious fruits that will soon be ready to eat.

I've tried to plant fruit for all seasons in this tiny Kentish garden of England. Starting with rhubarb, through the berries and cherries, and on to orchard fruits through the plums, gages and apricots. Optimistically, I've also popped in a fig, a passion fruit vine and a persimmon, but am yet to harvest anything edible from these tender delicacies.

Fast disappearing from commercial orchards, the damson is a fruit to relish, and I'm lucky to have several scraggy trees in my garden. Suckers abound, and I plant them about

and give them to friends. Mine's probably a 'Merryweather' cross, with large dusky-bloomed fruit that can be eaten straight from the tree – most other damsons are mouth-puckeringly sour and need cooking, sugar and vanilla to make them palatable.

Almost forgotten fruits: mirabelles, cherry plums, damson, bullaces and sloes: there's a bonanza crop of stone fruits ready to harvest along the paths down to the sea, all sports, crosses and remnants of old orchards that were once farmed here. I try to categorise them, which is which, but I'm none the wiser. The wild ones seem to be versions of *Prunus insititia*, but the difference between bullaces and damsons is down to local folklore, traditional nomenclature, the shape of the fruit and the texture of the stone, rather than colour and taste.

Stone Fruits

WHILE FRUIT IS RIPENING all around you, now's the time to plan which new varieties to grow next year, so you can harvest fruit the year through. Would you like to grow cordons, flat against a wall or fence, or maybe even step-overs, instead of low fences? Trained fruit trees are a good way to add design and structure to your garden, and the bonus is lots of delicious fruit.

Make sure when you buy stone-fruit trees that they are either self-fertile or you have another to fertilise them. Much new work has been done to make them easier to grow in our climate. Growing peaches, apricots and nectarines used to be relegated to a special wall-mounted greenhouse, and under glass is still the best way to grow peaches and avoid peach leaf curl. New varieties of apricot are so good that they're grown commercially for profit. Greengages and damsons are ancient orchard fruits with tastes that take you right back to childhood and need to be preserved so that they aren't just relegated to memory.

Plums Galore

Originally from Greece, there are more varieties of plum than any other fruit. Some of the rare ancient varieties, 'Belle de Louvain', 'Bountiful', 'Algrove's Superb' and 'Yellow Magnum Bonum', are the domain of specialist heritage nurseries; others may live on, unrecognised, in gardens, while many have disappeared. Each has a peculiar flavour or characteristics that make them special to certain locations. Seek out varieties that have a history to your area and keep them alive for future generations.

Varieties: choose several so they ripen over a long season. 'Victoria' will fertilise most other types and is a good doer, having large fruits with red flushed skin. 'Opal' is earlier and nicer-flavoured. Grow the cherry plum 'Mirabelle de Nancy' for early blossom and nectar and for making clafoutis.

Plant during winter months. Plums do well on a heavy soil, which is why they proliferate here on Kent clay.

Water regularly as they like a moist soil, but they won't put up with waterlogged ones.

Feed with well-rotted farmyard manure in spring and a top
dressing of potash in late winter.

Mulch as above.

Prune lightly to thin the old wood in spring and summer, to
reduce risk of disease. Plums do well as pyramids and fans.
All fruit prunings make good kindling when dry.

Thin to ease congestion, and prop up heavily fruiting branches
so they don't snap.

Pick in August and September, leaving fruit to ripen on the
tree, then keep hand-picking to stop them falling on to the
ground. You may need a safe ladder (the Japanese three-
legged ones are best for fruit picking). And beware: you'll
be competing with wasps.

Gages

Honey-flavoured with a touch of tartness, the shop-bought
greengage is often a woolly disappointment. Grow your own
and eat as many as you can straight from the tree, and when
stuffed, pick the rest to poach and freeze. Add lemon juice when
jamming, and serve with toasted brioche dusted with cinnamon
sugar; or simmer in butter with cinnamon and top with toasted
almonds and oats for a breakfast treat.

Developed by Sir Thomas Gage in Suffolk at the end of the
eighteenth century from wild trees grown in France, the trees
are neat and rarely grow taller than 3.5 metres. Gages can be
cross-fertilised by plums.

Varieties: I can recommend: 'Oullins Golden Gage', a vigorous
tree with large flavoursome golden fruits. 'Reine Claude de
Bavay' ripens later, as does 'Cambridge'.

Plant gages during winter: they need a drier, warmer position
than most plums. Grow them in light soil that's well aerated,
against a south-facing wall in cooler areas.

Water often – do not let newly planted trees dry out.

Feed in spring.

Mulch to keep down weeds around the base.

Prune in late spring and early summer. Plums and gages fruit
on growth made the previous year and also on short spurs
that build up on old wood.

Thin in mid-May by removing any fruit that touches a neighbour to stop the rot.

Pick in August and September. Greengages crop fairly erratically, so enjoy them when you can.

Peaches

Picture a perfect peach with downy bloom and luscious curves, then imagine a bowlful on your kitchen table, picked at their prime from a tree in your garden. Up until a few years ago these exotic fruits were relegated to the hothouse, often blighted with leaf curl, and at best, their harvest was sporadic, but thankfully now there's a range of new disease-resistant cultivars that seem capable of dealing with the vagaries of our climate.

Most stone fruits produce their fragile flowers on bare branches, early in the season, when the risk of frost is high and garden pollinators prepared to brave the cold are few. The heroic bumblebee in his furry coat is best for this job. Encourage him with other tempting delicacies and comfortable habitat over winter. Most peaches are self-fertile, but pollen needs to be transferred from one flower to another, so without bees, use a paintbrush.

Varieties: the latest advancement in varieties is 'Avalon Pride', with high resistance to leaf curl and vigour able to resist frost. 'Duke of York' is fine-flavoured and 'Bonanza' grows well in a pot and can be brought inside to overwinter.

Plant in the autumn in well-drained, well-dug soil against a south-facing wall.

Water well.

Feed like most fruit trees, which need to be fed potassium and nitrogen in early spring. Sprinkle on Growmore, blood, fish and bone, or dried poultry manure.

Mulch annually to reduce competition from surrounding grass, or use a mulch mat for the first 5 years of the tree's life.

Prune to replace old shoots with new, by removing the top ends of higher branches to encourage growth in late winter, as peaches fruit on young new growth.

Thin fruits to one every 15cm in June, and protect them from wasps and birds.

ESSENTIAL VEG

Now's the time to taste as many varieties of tomato as you can, so that next year you'll know exactly which ones to plant and which ones to avoid.

- You can dry seed from heirloom tomatoes by scooping them out.
- Add water and leave to ferment in a jar covered in cling film in which you've punched holes.
- Rinse them until the water runs clear, then sieve and dry for 2 weeks on a paper plate.
- Label and leave in a paper envelope until next April.
- Sow in an 8cm pot and keep the soil moist but not waterlogged.
- Pot on as they grow, and bring outside as danger of frost passes.
- Tomatoes are hungry plants, so feed regularly and keep them well watered.

Pick fruit that ripens naturally in the sun. This fruit, which is hand-picked at just the right time, depending on the weather (it should come away in the hand with a gentle lift), wins hands down over commercially grown and stored fruit.

Reward your efforts with a Bellini, made from a glass of blended peach nectar topped up with champagne or prosecco.

Apricots

With warmer springs and longer summers, apricots are the fruits of the future. Hardy trees, they don't even mind a cold winter, but what they don't like is variations in temperature. I've been growing abundant crops for the past ten years, and every summer we bottle, jam and gorge ourselves.

Varieties include cold-tolerant varieties produced by Canadian breeders: 'Tomcot' (a large, heavy cropper with red-flushed fruit), 'Flavorcot' and 'Goldcot' are hardy and productive.

Plant between November and March in well-drained soil in a sunny position, away from frost pockets. In cooler areas, grow on dwarf rootstock in pots that can be moved under glass to protect their pretty, early pale pink flowers.

Water during the early growing period.

Prune: for best results, fan train against a south-facing wall. Ready-trained trees are available from nurseries. Prune trained trees in late summer when sap flow is low. Cut back side-shoots to their main framework. Cut out dead wood in winter.

Thin clusters of apricots to singles or doubles.

Pick straight away as soon as they ripen in summer.

Damsons

Originally from Damascus and introduced by the Romans, the oval damson tastes strangely sharp and sweet at the same time.

Varieties that are most commonly grown include the almost black-fruited 'Farleigh' – originally found growing wild here in Kent; the almost plum-size 'Merryweather', with large hyacinth-blue fruits that are good to eat raw; and the ancient 'Westmoreland', a local variety that has its own website – lythdamsons.org.uk – and its own Damson Day in spring.

Plant: damsons are disease-free and will grow in almost any soil apart from pure peat or really heavy clay. They don't thrive in the shade, and competition results in leggy trees. The best way to propagate is to dig up suckers, which will usually fruit in 5 years.

Water newly planted suckers well until established.

Feed with an occasional spring seaweed drench.

Mulch all trees with garden compost for their first 5 years.

Prune very little. Best left alone, apart from removing dead or diseased wood.

Thin: many fruit trees lose a percentage of their crops in June – the June drop, where the tree naturally sheds excess. Heavy cropping branches may need support.

Pick quickly, before the birds realise they're ripe.

When cooking damsons, the stones float up to the surface and you can scoop them out with a slotted spoon.

TIMELY ADVICE

Lightly prune lavender once the bees have finished foraging.

Cut away yellowing leaves of courgettes and pumpkins so the fruits ripen.

Feed and water agapanthus and lilies in their pots after they've flowered.

Split irises, cutting their leaves in a fan shape so they don't dehydrate.

Clean out your poultry houses regularly in hot weather and freshen drinking water.

Group container plants together and water them all at the same time.

Any pots that have dried out need to be plunged into a bath full of water to soak.

Make sure your pigs' wallow is kept wet and that they have plenty of shade.

Keep goose and duck ponds topped up, and clean up regularly.

Celebrating in Your Garden

WHEN I WAS PLANNING my previous garden thirty-odd years ago, I can't remember dedicating such a large portion to outdoor eating – nearly a third of my new plot has been set aside just for the pleasure of garden meals. Perhaps in the meantime the weather really has got warmer; more likely I spend more time sitting down, or maybe we've really become a nation of al fresco diners.

Most garden furniture is hugely uncomfortable, so bring out lots of cushions and pretty up your table with patterned cloths – plasticated ones can stay out all summer. Make canopies and awnings with sheets clipped on to fences or poles and guy ropes. An outdoor storage chest is a good idea, so you can stash away things you don't want to get wet – especially if it doubles up as a bench.

As a family, we love to party outside. We've welcomed newcomers with tree planting ceremonies and hot toddies by fire-bowls; remembered the dearly departed with garden memorial sculptures and pet burials; celebrated birthdays, weddings and jubilees and given courses on how to make the most of your garden.

Opening your garden to the public is a great way to raise money for charities, and plant stalls are nearly as popular as cake stalls as fundraisers. Make sure your garden is as safe as it can be, and it's a good idea to plan a route for visitors so they don't get snarled up. I love visiting other people's gardens too, and enjoying what Vita Sackville-West called 'a shortcut to hard-won experience'.

Damsons in a Roast Hazelnut Crumble

You could also try baked apricots or plums with almond crumble, and, later in the season, blackberries and elderberries with apples in a walnut crumble.

Preheat the oven to 180°C/gas 4.

Stone enough damsons to cover the bottom of a buttered and sugar-dusted baking dish.

Pour in enough apple juice to cover the damsons and a teaspoon of vanilla essence.

Roast some hazelnuts in a single layer in a large pan on a hot stove. Stir frequently until the nuts start to turn brown, then remove from the pan.

Mix together enough crumble to cover the fruit, with porridge oats, the chopped roast hazelnuts and sugar to taste.

Add a teaspoon of ground cinnamon.

Moisten with walnut, hazelnut or olive oil.

Sprinkle the crumble over the fruit.

Bake in the oven for 40 minutes, until the topping is browned.

SEPTEMBER

HARVEST

Orchard Fruits

Autumn Veg

Eggstras: Guinea Fowl

Pickled Fennel

September

is my favourite month

of the whole year.

The summer's drought has broken; plants have a new lease of life and so do I, all of us basking in the low light that shows off the autumnal colours so effectively and increases mellow endorphins. Although you've probably been harvesting colander-fuls of bits and bobs of produce as it's been growing, all of a sudden, even the most well organised of gardeners can feel slightly overwhelmed with nature's bounty.

Brave the spiders' webs and go out every morning to see what's ripe and ready. Try to eat as many things as possible straight from the plant, because that's why you're growing your own – to have access to really fresh produce at its best. 'Eat fresh, store the excess, then give away as much as you can' should be your motto.

It may be worth warning friends and family that you'll be a pop-up greengrocer for the next few weeks.

Some frost-hardy vegetables will last quite happily if left growing in the soil: that's why I grow leeks, rather than onions. Pumpkins, squashes and gourds will ripen off the ground in a sunny spot until the first frosts; celery and celeriac will keep fresh with an overcoat of straw; and hearty kales and winter salads should be planted now.

Handle your produce carefully, then freeze, store or preserve straight away, before it loses its goodness. Label your harvest with a date and description – all frozen veg look the same in a bag, covered with frost. As you're harvesting, make notes for next year, reminding yourself that maybe you don't need to sow quite so

many courgette seeds, or that even your greedy flock of hens were rather overwhelmed with all that spinach.

It's worth remembering that although by law we're not supposed to give our poultry or pigs kitchen waste, any garden-grown leftovers can go straight into the run or pen, and pigs and ducks love windfalls. To add to nature's bounty, your poultry will start laying again after the moult, orchard fruit will be ripening, tomatoes, peppers, chillies and aubergines will be colouring up, and it'll soon be time to send off your pigs.

It is possible to grow plants of most produce in succession, but even a dwarf apple tree will provide too many apples to eat, and few friends thank you for a bag of apples – they're all wondering what to do with their own. Maybe sharing a juicer with neighbours would

solve the glut and justify the cost of kit that's used only once a year.

Think maybe how to extend your season by planting a few new fruit and veg varieties next year, or buy a greenhouse or cold frame so you can produce earlier and later varieties with a little extra heat, or grow more tender types of produce, and reduce the bog standard fruit and veg. Remember that your garden's wildlife will always appreciate what you grow, so leave plenty of leftovers for them to enjoy.

Orchard Fruits

THE APPLES AND PEARS in the UK are second to none, growing perfectly in our climate and embellishing the countryside and gardens during the flowering and fruiting season.

Apples

I inherited a lovely old standard apple tree, possibly a 'Grenadier', an early cropper with large, pale green fruit that's ready to eat or cook in August. The first apples to fall are not keepers, so you'll need to keep up or they'll go rotten and, of course, you shouldn't wait until they drop, or they'll bruise. Check if they're ready with a twist of the wrist – ripe fruit will come away easily.

To extend my apple picking season, I planted two 'Katy' cordoned apple trees grown along the fence – sentinels at the orchard gate with bright red, sweet fruit that ripens and should be eaten in late August – and a dwarf 'Red Falstaff', ripe and ready in September/October – a keeper I store and can still eat in January.

Varieties include earlies: 'Sunrise'; mid-seasons: 'Egremont Russet'; keepers: 'Cox's'. Cookers and eating apples are available on a variety of rootstocks, from tiny container size to massive standards, and can be trained as cordons, espaliers, step-overs or fans.

Store perfect apples. Space them carefully so they're not touching, in shallow cardboard fruit boxes (available free from shops and market stalls) in a cool, dark, well-ventilated shed or garage, away from vermin and onions, and check regularly, removing any that start to rot.

Preserve by stewing and freezing for sauces and pie fillings; making chutney or juicing using an electric juicer. The juice can be frozen in small plastic bottles.

Cook fritters with cinnamon; try freshly grated in breakfast muesli; caramelise with walnuts; mull with brandy and make into a remoulade with celeriac.

Pears

One of the features of my springtime garden is a venerable 'Doyenne du Comice' covered in blossom. Sadly, these flowers rarely turn to fruit, maybe due to its age, but I usually get a dozen or so juicy pears that almost melt in the mouth. I planted a dwarf 'Concorde' nearby: a new variety that gets its taste from its 'Comice' relations and its vigour from the 'Conference' side of the family.

Varieties: 'Williams' is a classic English pear, while 'Bosc' is best for cooking and poaching. Pear trees are often grown as espaliers against a warm wall.

Store in small cardboard trays because they tend to ripen at the same time. Check daily: pears change colour as they ripen. Bring them into a warm house (an airing cupboard is ideal) and when the top near the stalk is soft, they're ready to eat.

Preserve by drying pear rings that have been coated with lemon juice on a rack in the oven or dehydrator, or juice and freeze.

On warm days you can ripen pears on a sunny windowsill, but keep an eye open for foraging wasps.

Cook by poaching in red wine with vanilla, star anise or cardamom. Pears are also delicious with melted dark chocolate.

Quinces

My quince tree, *Cydonia* 'Champion', has the prettiest sugar-pink blossom, shapely leaves that turn yellow in autumn and downy lime-green fruits that turn butter-yellow as they ripen. I also grow *Chaenomeles japonica* flat against the fence and these produce smaller quinces, but their flowers are showier. Quinces like a moist rich soil in a sunny spot.

Varieties: 'Vranja' grows enormous fruit like boulders on an upright tree, and 'Lescovac' is a prolific fruiter.

Store away from apples and pears or the quince will taint their taste. I keep quinces in a blue bowl in the kitchen, where they scent the room.

Preserve: I bake quinces in the oven until soft, then scoop out the flesh and freeze. This saves on peeling and chopping – no mean feat, as many quinces are as hard as rocks even when ripe.

Cook them stuffed in your Christmas goose, and add them to any dish where you'd normally use apples during late autumn. Because of their high pectin content, quinces make lovely jewel-like jelly. If you're feeling energetic, grate quince into brandy with sugar and leave to turn into a ruby-red liqueur.

Crab Apples

Grow a crab apple for its beauty and as a present to your garden's wildlife. The leaves are food to many moth caterpillars, the flowers provide a pretty early source of pollen, and most garden birds and mammals love the fruits that hang on late into winter. The wood smells lovely when burning, too, so save prunings for kindling.

Varieties: some crab apples have green leaves with pale pink blossom, while others are bronze-leaved with darker pink blossom. Fruits vary from yellow, orange and red to crimson and dark maroon. 'John Downie' is considered the best for cooking; the fruits of 'Golden Hornet' and 'Comtesse de Paris' last a long time on the tree; and 'Laura' is columnar, with bronze leaves and large red fruit.

Store what you need and leave the rest on the tree for the birds, to hang like small Christmas decorations late into winter.

Cook jelly to go with roast meats and game; add a few to the roasting pan with game birds and their juice will flavour the gravy; or add to hot cider wassail punches instead of apple rings.

Autumn Veg

DON'T LET YOUR VEGETABLE PLOT stand empty over winter. There's a bowlful of salad leaves, a rainbow of hardy kales and a range of tangy onions that you should plant now and that will grow right into winter – and if it's a mild one, most plants, including the multi-coloured chards and rockets (try mildew-resistant 'Athena') go on growing well into November and December. You can plant broad beans and peas now for a good start, but they'll need staking over winter.

Kales

These glamorous denizens of the winter veg patch will provide colour and goodness throughout the cold months. Try 'Red Russian', navy-blue cavolo nero, and grey-blue curly kale. Try the tiny central leaflets in salads, or strip larger leaves from their centre stem and eat them steamed or deep-fried. Kales are low in calories, high in fibre and full of vitamins – a nutritional powerhouse that keeps on growing whatever the weather. Much-loved by pigeons and other feathered friends, it's essential to protect this veg, or you'll be left with just their leafy skeletons.

Salads

Winter purslane or claytonia pops up self-seeded every autumn when I clear the bed of the remains of summer salads. I use the

TIMELY ADVICE

Give your flock a protein boost with pumpkin and sunflower seeds after the moult.

Cover autumn salads and vegetables with cages to protect from hungry pigeons and poultry.

Collect and store vegetable and flower seeds on a dry sunny day – pop them into envelopes and label them straight away.

Order bulbs so they'll be with you in time to plant in October.

leaves, packed full of vitamin C, in mixed salads. Chinese tatsoi can be cooked whole, or individual leaves harvested for stir-fries. Corn salad 'Verte de Cambrai' has small tasty leaves that add flavour to winter salads, and mustard 'Red Giant' or 'Ruby Streaks' leaves pack a real punch with a fiery flavour. Just add a few to liven up cooked and raw dishes.

Lamb's lettuce is a useful bulking leaf in the salad bowl and can be sown outside until the end of next month.

Perpetual Spinach

This leafy green is actually a chard, but has a spinach flavour and will keep going over winter if you remove the outer leaves to allow space for new growth and to improve its flavour. This robust plant prefers to grow in colder weather, and doesn't mind a little shade. Strip out the stems and wash the leaves well before cooking, then steam as ordinary spinach – delicious as a bed for a poached newly-laid egg topped with a grating of Parmesan and a little black pepper.

Onions & Leeks

My Welsh onions seem to carry on regardless of temperature. Winter-hardy varieties of spring onions planted now will be ready by early spring. Leeks are at their best from November to April, but I grow a row or two all year round. I leave a few to flower and always have my own seed, a row of tiny seedlings and another line of larger ones, ready to eat. Delicious steamed with red peppers or chargrilled with courgettes, leeks are the most versatile vegetable in the winter plot.

Eggstras: Guinea Fowl

IF I'VE BEEN UNABLE to tempt you with ducks, quail, hens or geese (see pages 34, 63, 70 and 184), perhaps guinea fowl will do the trick. Like a crocodile of meek convent girls in pale grey uniforms, a small flock of guinea fowl will wander round your garden together, pecking up grass, bugs and grubs, but leaving vegetables for you and your family. In spotty buffs, greys, bronzes and mauves, these free-range birds will raise the alarm at strangers, but their constant twittering (by day and by night) will test the patience of a saint.

Originally from the African veldt, they are wilder than other poultry and prefer to roost high in the trees and lay in the garden, unless you buy them young and tempt them under cover into their house every night with a corn supper. Guinea fowl are good all-rounders, laying 50–100 brown spotted eggs a year for breakfast and making a tasty game supper too, and they'll live happily alongside other garden poultry.

Never remove all their eggs from the nest, or they'll stop laying or find a new nesting site, and you'll need all your ingenuity to find it. Guinea fowl eggs are 30% smaller than hen's, with a good ratio of yolk to whites, very hard shells and a rich creamy flavour. Their beautiful feathers are in demand from fly fishermen.

TIMELY ADVICE continued

Plant indoor hyacinth bulbs in a cool dark place and bring them on to a windowsill about a fortnight before Christmas when you want them to flower.

Keep picking flowers, veg, herbs and salads little and often, just enough for a meal.

Order mushroom kits. Try out some new varieties (see page 176).

It will soon be time to send your pigs off. Get in touch and book in with your chosen slaughterhouse and butcher.

Pickled Fennel

PICKLED VEG ADDS A TART NOTE and a bit of excitement to autumn dishes.

Chop a bulb of fennel very finely.

Pop it into a bowl of water with 2 teaspoons of salt and leave for an hour.

Rinse and pack into a well-washed jar.

Boil together ½ a cup of cider vinegar and ½ a cup of water.

Add a tablespoon of honey and 2 teaspoons of fennel seeds.

Bring to the boil, cool, then pour the liquid over the fennel, making sure it is completely covered.

Keep in the fridge; it improves with time, but use within a week.

OCTOBER

PIGS & FUNGI

Keeping a Couple of Pigs
in Your Garden

Mushrooms

Mushrooms on Toast

A bright October
is a bonus;
it prolongs the season.

And even though dusk starts to come earlier in October, it also means longer lie-ins in the mornings. Every day, it's my livestock that gets me up and out of bed, and after feeding the cat, the hen house is my first port of call with a mug of tea in hand.

Hens can't see in the dark and will conveniently make their own way to roost at dusk and stay sleeping until dawn, so it's pointless trying to get them up before daylight. For their security, ducks and geese can see in the dark – they can't roost in trees, so they often sleep with one eye open. Pigs also wake with the sun, and hungry piglets like an early breakfast.

I no longer have the space or neighbours who would take kindly to a serious small-holding, but many gardeners find being a fair-weather pig-keeper (buying a few piglets, growing them over summer, then taking them to slaughter in the autumn) is a rewarding introduction to animal husbandry and a tasty way of producing homegrown protein.

There's plenty to eat for all animals at this time of the year, as they fatten themselves up for the winter ahead. The feathered contingency is pecking at seeds, nuts and fruit, while pigs are enjoying chestnuts, acorns, apples, blackberries and even stinging nettles, roots and all. Squirrels, mice and other tiny furry creatures are all enjoying the fruits of your labours, so make sure you don't tidy your flowerbeds and hedges until early spring.

With harvest mostly over, it's the beginning of the gardening year. Time to re-seed your

lawn, pot bulbs, plant perennials, biennials and sow spring bedding, and a good time to settle or move trees, shrubs and climbers. The leaves are beginning to fall, ready to be swept up into builders' bags and rot down for leaf mould, but I only clear the paths and lawn – the rest are left in situ to shelter overwintering wildlife.

Kicking around the fallen leaves, you may come across mushrooms or toadstools. The well-versed mycologist may even forage them for breakfast, but safer perhaps to grow your own – indoors or outside, in the scullery or on the compost heap. Like most homegrown crops, they taste much better than shop-bought.

With Christmas decorations in mind, I will have started to squirrel away leaves, seed heads, cones and dried flowers. My kitchen table looks like a primary-school nature table, with pumpkins heralding the first of the winter celebrations, designed to keep us upbeat and busy throughout the fallow season.

Keeping a Couple of Pigs in Your Garden

So you've decided to keep a few pigs. Start the process now by doing the necessary paperwork, and you will be ready to buy two weaners (6–8-week-old piglets) in the spring, letting them enjoy the summer in your garden and taking them off to slaughter in the autumn. Because they're only with you over the summer, your ground won't be spoiled, and as my friend, smallholder Karen Nethercott, says, 'From the moment we unloaded our first squealing weaners, to the pleasurable hours spent making salamis, I've loved every minute. I fell in love with my pigs, and yes, I missed them when they went, but if you eat pork, surely it is better to eat animals you know have lived a really good life?'

If you want to keep pigs to eat, there are several bureaucratic hurdles you'll have to jump.

- Locate a nearby abattoir that accepts private kills. Make sure they will take most pigs, as some are fussy about breeds.
- Next, contact your local Environmental Health office to check if there are any contra-indications to you keeping pigs.
- Make sure your property deeds don't preclude keeping livestock.
- Then your next step will be to register with and get a holding number and a herd number from DEFRA.
- Finally, call your local Trading Standards and ask them to send you some blank movement licences and a movements book. They will tell you what records you need to keep.
- Have a word with your neighbours. Living next door to a couple of pigs may not be everyone's cup of tea.

While you're waiting for your paperwork to arrive, you can enjoy yourself deciding which breed of pigs to keep. The Rare Breeds Survival Trust's website is a joy to visit, and the delights of each breed are celebrated. I've narrowed the field to my top six breeds on page 170–171. Once you decide, contact the relevant Breed Club or your local county Smallholding Group and they'll put you in touch with nearby herds with weaners for sale.

Stash away your prettiest produce to use to decorate your house and celebrate the changing seasons (left).

Always visit the litter before you buy, and never buy a single pig – they're friendly creatures that need a pal, but make sure your choices are the same sex. Don't get too attached to them or give them names, unless they are of a culinary nature: Bacon and Sausage are favourites. Piglets are captivating and you'll probably hate 'sending them off', especially the first time, but remember, they arrive as adorable toddlers and leave as belligerent teenagers.

Set up your paddock in advance and remember that your charges will need to be fed twice a day, have access to water and shelter, and their quarters will need to be cleaned out once a week, though pigs, despite their reputation, are not dirty.

Where to Keep Your Pigs

The ideal home is a piece of woodland or orchard at least 20 metres square per pair of piglets or per adult pig – if it's populated with edible trees, like the sweet chestnuts in these photographs, it will be piggy paradise. Light sandy soil is best, but if it's a temporary summer let, any site will do. Pigs make light work of any undergrowth and will rootle away, so if it's land you want cleared, so much the better.

Pigs soon learn to respect an electric fence, so keep them contained with two strands of wire at about 15cm and 30cm off the ground. Use a system with plastic posts, and walk the perimeter every day to make sure the bottom strand doesn't get covered with mud, and the surrounding grass hasn't grown up.

A pig ark is a thing of beauty, made of traditional corrugated iron, sturdy and moveable; try to find one with an insulated roof that will keep its occupants warm at night. Keep your ark topped up with straw, and make sure the entrance points away from prevailing winds. Pigs don't soil their house, but mud gets everywhere, so a regular change of bedding is recommended.

Make sure there's a shady area for pigs to keep out of the summer sun. If there are no trees, rig up a tarpaulin, making sure the posts are pig-proof. Pigs don't sweat and easily overheat, so a wallow is really important – it cools them down and acts as a sunscreen. Run a hosepipe into a slight dip in the ground and top it up every other day so they can enjoy a good mud bath.

Which Breed?

Most pigs you see in commercial units are Prick-eared Whites. Fifty years of selective breeding has created an animal that produces a battery of uniform piglets that are early to wean and quick to fatten – great for cheap meat, but not so good for tasty meat, and often dry with rubbery crackling.

At the beginning of the twentieth century there were still lots of regional pig breeds, selectively bred to suit local conditions, until the government decided to focus on breeds suited to intensive factory farming. The traditional breed numbers fell dramatically, some disappearing altogether. The turning point came in 1973 with the setting up of the Rare Breeds Survival Trust. Since then, not a single breed of British farm animal has become extinct, and with the help of local breed clubs, numbers are increasing.

By choosing rare breeds, you become part of this success story. Try one breed now and another next year, and you'll notice the difference in looks, temperament and, above all, in the taste and texture of their meat. You'll soon have a favourite, and may want to start breeding your own herd. Encouragement to eat rare breeds may seem a contradiction in terms, but it's only by eating them that the genetic pool increases.

British Saddleback

BRITISH SADDLEBACK

Resulting from the amalgamation of the Essex and the Wessex, this is a hardy, problem-free pig and an excellent mum. These are good starter pigs, good for both pork and bacon.

GLOUCESTER OLD SPOT

Known as the Orchard Pig, their spots are said to have been caused by falling apples! Hardy and well suited to outdoor life, these are the friendliest, most docile pigs, but their skin is prone to sunburn, so a wallow and shelter are essential.

Gloucester Old Spot

TAMWORTH

Originating in the Midlands, this is the only British red pig and the truest indigenous breed, retaining the long snout of the earliest types. This prick-eared breed is a mischievous handful, but is a good bacon pig because of its length.

Tamworth

LARGE BLACK

Britain's only black pig, this is a friendly, docile lop-eared breed that makes a good mum with large litter sizes. The meat is valued for its succulence. No worries about sunburn either.

MIDDLE WHITE

A rather ugly small white pig with a pug nose and prick ears that matures quickly and has a reputation for top-quality pork. The breed has a number of high-profile fans among celebrity chefs, who sing the praises of its succulent meat.

Large Black

KUNE KUNE

Kune Kunes come from New Zealand, and these delightfully chubby animals are a great option for those who just want to keep pigs as lifetime pets, rather than for the table. Small (60–75cm high), they come in a range of colours, love human company and do less damage in the garden, where they graze rather than root.

Middle White

What To Feed Your Pigs

Pigs' table manners leave a lot to be desired. Feed them twice a day straight from the ground, because they'll flip most drinkers and feeders over. Rotate their feeding area so it doesn't get fouled.

Invest in a nipple drinking system, available from agricultural merchants. It's easy to

Kune Kune

run and best for the pigs, who need fresh drinking water at all times. Stand the barrel on a sheet of plywood to stop the pigs making a wallow underneath and tipping the container over.

Pigs will eat almost anything you put in front of them, so make sure it's safe. They'll thrive on any surplus produce from the veg garden and orchard, even grass clippings. Remember the golden rule – absolutely no meat, fish or kitchen waste.

While any bonuses will be appreciated, the easiest way to make sure your charges are getting a good balanced diet is to feed them pelleted pignuts, sold in 20kg bags from agricultural feed merchants. Avoid those based on fishmeal, because it taints the meat.

A bag of pignuts will feed 2 weaners for about 2 weeks, but by the time they reach 5 months, it will disappear in a week, depending on how much extra veg you feed them. A kilo of veg is worth half a kilo of pignuts.

Raising Piglets

Once you feel you've mastered the art of raising weaners and want to progress to breeding your own, you'll need a lot more space to keep them in and more time to look after them. Two facts are worth remembering: adult pigs can live for 10–15 years and they produce litters of about 20 piglets a year, so will you be able to market them or their meat? Just one 8-month-old pig will provide you with about 120 portions of meat.

If these facts don't deter you, then please go on a course and learn how to become an advanced pig-keeper. You'll need to decide whether to keep a boar (they can be problematic), borrow a boar or go in for artificial insemination, and you'll also have to learn which sows to breed from (nipple count rates high), how to deal with pregnant mums, labour and farrowing houses, and how to look after tiny piglets.

Gardening with Pigs

Pigs make the best land clearers, eating every known weed and garden plant, but don't let them have access to hemlock, henbane, foxglove, bracken, ivy, laburnum, ragwort or yew. Lucy Adams, who gardens at Doddington Place, and looks after the Sandy

ESSENTIAL VEG

Asparagus is a luxury veg that's best eaten straight from the plot. You need a little extra space, but I used to use the rest of my bed to grow courgettes, once the asparagus had been picked.

- If you plant asparagus crowns now, you'll get an earlier crop next year.
- Pick a weed-free site in a raised bed that's well mulched.
- Dig a 15cm wide trench that's 20cm deep.
- Straddle the crowns over the ridge 45cm apart and cover with 10cm of soil.
- Water well and keep weed-free.
- Do not harvest for the first 2 years, but cut down the foliage in autumn.
- Never harvest asparagus spears after the middle of June.

and Blacks in these photos, says they put all their garden detritus into the pig run and most of it disappears.

Pigs are amazingly strong, so anything you put into their sty will be manhandled and moved. Give them a log or two or a rubber tyre to play with. Trees will need their bark protected. Pigs will rub against trees and browse low-level leaves and twigs. Pig-proof tree guards made of strong timber and wire will be needed to protect young and slender trees.

Stack spent bedding on a covered compost heap, layered with pig manure and green material, turn it every 3 months and leave for at least a year or over winter. It can be a bit smelly to start with, so make sure your heap is well away from neighbours' boundaries. It is less rich than poultry manure, but you could try selling excess at the garden gate.

Possible Problems

Piglets are normally wormed when they are weaned, so check this has been done when you buy and you won't have to medicate them again during their stay with you.

If you do, then administer wormer and remember to record any medication in your records.

The combination of piggy ballerina points and uneven ground often results in the odd limp. It usually sorts itself out in the end. If not, a visit to the vet may be in order. Most fair-weather pig-keepers rarely encounter health problems with their pigs. Providing you buy healthy stock from a trusted source, rare breeds tend to be hardy, and by keeping them outdoors in a natural habitat with plenty of space, you'll be giving them a stress-free environment in which they'll thrive.

Pork

It can be difficult to send your first weaners to the abattoir, but it helps to have your friendly face accompanying them. When you've made an appointment with the abattoir, get them used to the trailer by leaving it in their paddock with the ramp down for a couple of days, and feed them inside. They'll probably be inside waiting for you on their last day, and all you need to do is shut the door behind them.

Mark your stock with your herd number by slap-marking them on each shoulder with an inkpad and slap pin, available from smallholder supplies. Take your completed movement licence with you to the abattoir and fill in the abattoir's Food Chain Information Form (FCI).

You can butcher the carcass yourself if the meat is for home consumption and you've been on a course to learn how to do it, but the most usual route is to arrange for the abattoir or a trustworthy local butcher to cut up the meat to your specifications – check his range first, especially his sausages. This may be the spur it takes for you to learn to do it yourself. Incidentally, all pigs have white skin after slaughter.

Mushrooms

WHAT COULD BE TASTIER to go with a good plate of home-reared sausages than a dish of homegrown mushrooms? And this is the perfect time to grow them, when it's cool and damp.

Mushrooms aren't magic, they're the fruits of a perennial underground network of mycelium cells, grown to release spores to reproduce themselves. They are packed with vitamins and minerals, but low in calories – though they absorb oil, butter and cream readily. You can try several varieties that are easy to grow:

Oyster mushrooms come in several colours, with gills running off their centre stems, and are delicately flavoured with a velvety texture. They grow fast, especially in spring and autumn. Great stir-fried, but use them quickly – they don't keep.

King oysters have a tan cap on a stout white stem. They keep firm when cooked and have a sweet woody flavour. Delicious eaten on toast, as fresh as possible.

Shitake are much sought after – they have a

rich, smoked, woody, meaty taste in soups and risottos, and are almost impossible to overcook. They have a large brown spongy cap, and the stems are a bit chewy – keep them to flavour soups.

Chestnut mushrooms are an earthier version of the common white buttons, with pinkish gills. I like them raw, with a lemony salad dressing. They grow prolifically from a kit. Grown larger, they turn into portobellos, but grown indoors in the heat, they soon spread their spores and disintegrate.

Many seed companies sell fresh mushroom spawn in windowsill box kits, in straw kits in bin liners, on hardwood logs or in wooden dowels that you plant in compost in the soil. All kits come with easy-to-follow instructions on how and where to keep your kit, and how to water and feed them to produce the best results. Always store your mushroom harvest in a paper bag in the fridge, but best to eat them fresh.

Mushrooms on Toast

THIS DISH MAKES a hearty breakfast or a tasty light lunch or supper dish.

Chop a few mushrooms and cook them slowly in olive oil with a little garlic.

Add a spoonful of crème fraîche, season with salt and pepper and remove from the heat.

Fry a slice of Parma or Ibérico ham in the same pan.

Toast a slice of sourdough bread.

Stack the mushrooms on the toast, then add the ham and a sprinkle of chopped parsley, with a little winter savory.

Serve straight away.

TIMELY ADVICE

Plant bulbs now: in the soil, in grass, in pots and in rows in the cutting garden.

Clear out your seed box of old packets. Scatter annuals into the beds and veg seeds into a seed tray for a last harvest of micro-greens before the frosts set in.

Plant sweet pea seeds in trainers and pop in a sheltered place.

Collect new seed as it ripens on the plant. Store in brown paper bags in a dry spot.

Check your stored fruit and remove any rotten ones.

Leave pumpkins, squash and gourds to dry off the ground in a sunny spot.

Make sure your winter veg is netted for protection from pigeons and other pests.

If you don't get back until after dark, invest in an automatic feeder for poultry suppers, or you'll find they've gone off to bed on empty stomachs.

NOVEMBER

GEESE

Geese: Where to Begin

Pumpkin Soup
with Roast Pumpkin Seeds
and Walnut Pesto

At dim and misty first light,

I skirt the nut trees to harvest

what the squirrels have left.

Mostly the walnuts come away from their shells with a swift kick of a boot. Best not to use your hands – the skins stain and no amount of scrubbing will clean them. An orange stick dipped in a little diluted bleach works wonders on your fingernails if you have to look tidy.

Every afternoon, just before the hens are fed, I sweep up the leaves under the walnut tree to stop the rotting leaves and nut casings killing the grass, and keep the paths clear to prevent slipping. A bit of a chore, but beneficial for the waistline and energetic heart massage. The bonus is inhaling that heavenly smell. Generally, though, leaves can be left to rot down in beds and borders.

In the meantime, spring-hatched pullets will start to lay (their first egg is often the size of a blackbird's), while my older bantams have stopped laying. One is moulting her pretty feathers late, and looking chilly as she braves the gusty winds. Now is the time to batten down the hatches and make sure your stock has adequate shelter from draughts and cold winds – strategically placed straw bales will make their lives easier.

While I bring a few seed heads into the house for decoration, I leave my garden to quietly rot down alone, leaving stems for insects to overwinter, piles of logs and stones to offer shelter, and berries and rotting fruit as winter feed for small mammals and birds. A tidy garden is no good to anyone, and the winter garden has a beauty of its own.

Overhead, skeins of wild geese are already arriving in the estuary. Domestic geese aren't really garden poultry. They're more at home on smallholdings, in paddocks and orchards with a quarter acre of grassland at least, plus access to water. Both are a must before considering these beguiling creatures. Sadly I now no longer have the sort of acreage sufficient to entertain even a pair, but the stories my sources tell make me long to feel the same affinity. Goose owners really love their geese.

Once a common sight, the sentinels at every farm gate, I still pass one small flock regularly and it cheers me to see them – gander with head held high – daring all comers to approach, while his wives busily graze their patch of grass. Producers of gargantuan grade A eggs and premium home-reared meat, geese supply top-grade fertiliser, soil conditioner and com-

post activator. They're maintenance-free lawn mowers, honk a strident alarm audible to the entire neighbourhood, and will entertain the whole family (though I'd never trust a goose with small children). Geese are easy to keep, but you need space, and above all, because they are long-lived, you need commitment.

Geese: Where to Begin

MICHAELMAS WAS THE TIME when geese were sent to market. Fully grown and fattened up on autumn harvests, they provided the celebratory meals of the season. Perhaps you have the space and long-term commitment to give a few geese a home?

First check your deeds to see if there are reasons not to keep poultry on your land. Then have a word with your neighbours: your honking flock of avian neighbourhood watch will alert the whole county. Geese are the cheapest of lodgers, but the large breeds are expensive to buy, especially the ornamentals, so stick to the smaller breeds we recommend on pages 188–189.

Finding your first gaggle will be fun. Visit local shows, charm waterfowl friends for surplus stock and scan the smallholder magazines and websites for breeders. The Domestic Waterfowl Club and Goose Club will recommend, but always inspect stock, ordering well beforehand, and have your pen, shelter and feed ready and waiting before you collect in early winter. Pairing starts in early autumn, so check your pair are, in fact, a pair.

Adopt a routine that suits you both. Your flock should be fed in the morning in their pen, let out to graze, potter, preen and doze until sunset, then encourage back to their quarters for supper and bed. You can also leave them to a totally free-range existence, like smallholder Rosemary Jordan does with her flock of thirty or so Embden crosses, featured in these photographs, especially if you have rolling acres as she does, but foxes will take their toll.

Geese are hardy, easy and great fun to keep, but remember that you'll need to feed them, clean their shelter regularly and visit them every day. They live for many years, so adopting a flock can be a commitment, but long-term connections can be hugely fulfilling.

Where to Keep Your Geese

Geese can see in the dark and will doze with one eye and half their brain alert to predators, but you must still protect your flock from foxes and uncontrolled dogs, especially if they can't fly because they're jumbo-sized or have clipped wings.

Their ideal home is a shed or shelter in the middle of a netted pen, leading to a paddock, field or orchard with a pond or riverbank. Keep them penned for the first few weeks until they know their address. Be warned, geese are major escapologists, so lighter breeds may need the first few flight feathers on one wing trimmed. Ask your breeder to do this.

If you're lucky enough to have moving water, remember that you'll have to net the area right down to the riverbed with galvanised netting to stop your flock sailing away. Visiting wildfowl will always be a nuisance, by interbreeding and stealing food. Of course, it is possible to keep geese without water, but although they aren't as aquatic as ducks, it would be hard to deny them a small pond at least. They love to paddle in and out, and preen, and some of the larger breeds need the extra buoyancy for successful mating.

Concrete or simply shaped fibreglass ponds (at least 30cm deep in the middle) can be cleaned with a broom and hose run to overflow. Water levels will have to be topped up daily in hot weather. If you're excavating a pond, use a strong liner and fold

Embden geese are handsome creatures; they'll act as neighbourhood watch and lay gargantuan eggs.

sturdy plastic netting round the turf edges to stop the perimeter being dabbled away. Alternatively protect banks with flints, logs or angled flagstones.

Fence your pen, especially if you live in a foxy area, making use of a strong electric fence, and build your shelter in the middle. Geese are hardy. Keep them under cover at night and you'll sleep better too, knowing they're safe from predators. House them at about a square metre per bird with a large door access – unlike other poultry, geese are wary of pop-holes and won't go in to sleep or lay. They don't roost, so above head height is only useful to you for easy access mucking out. If you have to crouch, you'll be less likely to carry out cleaning duties.

Make sure the floor is kept dry or its occupants will develop arthritic legs. Cover the floor with a thick layer of straw or corrugated cardboard bedding (available from your feed merchant) and replace when damp. The sweepings will rot down nicely on your compost heap.

You may want to herd your flock into a barn on winter nights, and if your geese come to you determinedly free-range and unused to being housed, then at least pen them at night in safety in a large portable rigid wire dog cage, encouraging them in with a handful of corn or herding them with whip sticks. They can be trained with patience: think of all those fairytale goose girls.

Choosing Your Geese

Domestic geese have evolved from various wild species whose chevrons in the sky magically augur winter. Some breeds were developed to lay, but few lay more than a large clutch in spring; the white ones were bred to supply feathers and down; but most, especially the massive Toulouse, were destined for the table.

Always popular on mixed farms because of their self-sufficiency, geese would be fattened up on stubble grass and would gobble up orchard windfalls, to be offered as Michaelmas rent to the landowner. The rest were then plumped up on grain and driven to the Christmas markets.

A goose is a multi-purpose bird. Historic recipes for goose fat abound: it was rubbed to get a shine on metal pots, prescribed as a poultice for invalids, as hand cream for dairymaids, as lotion for cows' udders and for babies with chapped lips.

In the tack room, it was smeared on harness and leather, rubbed on sheepdogs' paws, and anointed to highlight beaks and legs by proud poultry showmen.

The curled feathers were used as fishing tackle, the flights to steady arrows and the quills of artists. Housemaids removed dust from velvet with stiff plumes, and goose down is the softest filling for pillows and duvets. Goose was especially popular meat during the war, when feeding animals with food fit for human consumption was banned and flocks could fend for themselves.

Starting from scratch, I suggest you buy two females of one of the smaller breeds, then hatch out a few goslings from brought-in hatching eggs over the next few years, to bring your flock up to the sort of numbers your land can cope with. Keep one gander from your hatchings, bearing in mind that pairs mate for life and pine miserably if separated. The heavier birds do best in trios, but a smaller gander can manage up to six ladies.

Embden

EMBDEN (GERMANY) 14kg
A huge snow-white shapely bird, upright and handsome, with orange beak and legs – the goose of fairytales. Valued for its white down, they make good mums, but only lay 20 eggs a year. Effective burglar alarm, with a strident call.

TOULOUSE (FRANCE) 10kg
Bruiser of the goose world, with a low-slung keel and triple chin, bred unsurprisingly for the table. Docile, with majestic bulk, shouldn't be allowed to get too paunchy or will suffer. Give plenty of opportunity for exercise.

Toulouse

PILGRIM (GB) 7kg
Charming bird with tiptoe upright stance, taken to America by the Pilgrim Fathers. The gander is white and his lady is grey with a black and white back. Young are easy to sex (males yellow, females grey) and easy to raise. Docile, quiet and small.

Pilgrim

CHINESE (ASIA) 5kg

A light, shapely goose with a graceful swanlike appearance that lays up to 100 eggs a year and sits well. Needs protection from the cold. White with orange beak or grey/brown with a black beak. Gander is especially noisy.

BRECON BUFF (WALES) 8kg

Medium-sized goose that lays well. Bred in Wales in the 1930s, both sexes are buff-coloured with nice chocolate markings and pink accessories. Docile and a good layer, this is a forager that does well in colder climates.

ROMAN (ITALY) 6kg

A small, chubby, pure white goose with impressive fertility and strong maternal instincts. Neat, active and nippy, with pinkish legs and bill, excellent for smaller gardens and a first-class beginner's bird.

Chinese

What to Feed Your Geese

Basically, geese need grass, grain, grit and water to survive. They are herbivores (not omnivores like most other poultry) and need large amounts of good grazing supplemented with helpings of mixed corn. A flock works well in a mixed smallholding, grazing much shorter grass than other stock. Your gaggle will flourish in an orchard, hoovering up windfalls. They won't thrive on really rough pasture, so when grass loses its goodness (between October and April), substitute grass for other greenery such as brassicas, along with extra corn and pellets. Beware, geese mess a lot, so don't encourage back-door snacks or feed them outside their run.

Brecon Buff

Offer grain in a sturdy trough in their pen for 20 minutes when you get up and then again at sunset, and leave your flock to top up with grass. Don't leave food about or it will attract other diners. If you want lots of eggs, feed 80% mixed corn to 20% goose pellets, available from your feed merchant. Take care not to drop those plastic twines from feed sacks, or they'll

Roman

be playfully gobbled up with dire results. Avocados, eucalyptus and chocolate are poisonous to geese.

Galvanised drinkers and feeders are more robust than plastic, except during icy weather when a plastic washing-up bowl will do the trick. Grit, needed for digestion, is naturally available in your garden soil, but supply it if for any reason your birds are confined. Keep all feed in dustbins with metal lids to deter rats, and make sure any leftovers are removed.

Eggs & Goslings

If you want to hatch from your own stock, a goose doesn't need a gander to produce eggs, just fertile ones, which you can buy in from breeders. Encourage her to lay indoors by boarding the darkest end of her shelter with a plank to provide a roomy nesting area. Fill with a comfy layer of straw and add a couple of large china eggs to encourage her to lay. Pick up any eggs you find lying about, to discourage vermin.

You can take eggs for the kitchen, but geese won't supply you consistently in the way ever-obliging hens do. You might get 80 eggs a year from a Chinese Brown, but of course goose eggs are much bigger, weighing in at a massive 200g each (as opposed to hen's eggs at 65g and duck eggs at 100g).

Geese usually lay every other morning, starting any time between mid-winter and mid-summer. Take them fresh from the nest box for cooking, but take care, a goose can be very protective of her clutch, to say nothing of the gander. Excellent in quiches and custards, with a creamy flavour, but the whites won't whip up for meringues or soufflés.

If you decide to augment your flock, remember that geese are xenophobic and unwelcoming to newcomers, though breeders say pairs of single ladies of breeding age are usually accepted, so the easiest way to raise numbers is to hatch. You can incubate, with around a 50% success rate, but youngsters without a mother to support them will have to be segregated until they can hold their own. Hatching your own is a good way to build up stock, but be patient: first-time mums are usually unsuccessful.

Leave any eggs your goose lays in the nest box, but not too many – she'll probably cover 6 easily. If you want to try a new breed or need new blood, buy in fertile eggs from a breeder and

ESSENTIAL VEG

Garlic is an essential health-giving kitchen ingredient, and you can use the chopped leaves like chives.

- Grow in an open, sunny site, in light, well-drained soil.
- Plant the cloves now and it will be ready to harvest in June.
- Gently push into the soil with the pointy end upwards, just below the soil's surface.
- Lift as the foliage yellows and dry off the ground, in the sun.

set them under her at night. She'll line her nest with down plucked from her breast and carefully cover her eggs when she nips out to feed. Make sure she has easy access to food, enough water to immerse her head, and clear away mess daily.

The incubation period is 30–32 days from the time the mother started to sit. The goslings will take a nail-bitingly long time to chip their way out of the shell. They'll stay under mum for 2 days, surviving on food from the egg. Don't be disappointed if she fails – goose eggs have a low hatching rate.

The gander will pace the pen like an expectant father. He can be reunited with his family when she sees fit to bring them out. Goslings are gorgeous, but be careful, because both parents will be fiercely protective. Feed the babes little and often on gosling crumbs and chopped lettuce, and offer access to good short grass – they'll grow like wildfire. For the first 3 weeks, keep them away from open water. Unlike most birds, geese don't feed their young, except by enthusiastic example.

Ganders can live for 30 years. Bigger than their wives, they are aggressive and full of bravado, standing between you and their flock hissing with neck outstretched. A hiss is just a warning, but during the mating season geese are particularly bellicose – you may have to carry a stick. Please don't let children anywhere near the pen at this time. Excess ganders are often culled for Christmas. You'll find this hard to contemplate. Go on a course and learn how to dispatch; alternatively, you'll probably find a local butcher keen to come and take surplus stock – goose meat is luxury fare.

Gardening with Geese

The two major problems with geese as co-gardeners are their big feet, and the mess. Lawns can be kept clean with quick bursts from a high-speed hose, but I challenge anyone to deal with large amounts of goose poo. Keep them out of parts of the

garden you value or sit in with metre-high fences. Young trees will need their bark protected.

On the upside, geese love clover (tougher grasses, docks, thistles and nettles are not on the menu) and will keep grass down in rougher areas. They'll forage ditches, hedgerows and boggy areas with minimum soil compaction, and if you need a lake or pond cleared of excessive vegetation – call in your gaggle. Their droppings fertilise the soil, and their bedding and feathers make fertile compost when added to the heap, layered with other kitchen and garden waste.

Be wary of penning your flock with other garden familiars – geese are bullies, but on an open smallholding, most animals learn to avoid the belligerent elements.

Possible Problems

Geese are amazingly hardy creatures and thrive with little input from their owners. Give them lots of space and rotate their grazing to avoid land becoming worm-infested. Though largely resistant to parasites, if your birds aren't thriving, suspect worms and get a remedy from your vet or farm supplier.

Provide lots of clean water for preening to prevent eye problems. Waterfowl kept on hard surfaces with no opportunity to swim often suffer from corns and callouses and can develop arthritis in damp bedding. Geese moult in the autumn, filling your garden with feathers. In summer, make sure your flock has access to shady spots, because sunstroke is not uncommon.

Like all poultry, geese are difficult to catch. They always seem to anticipate exactly what you have in mind. You can catch geese in their shelter at night, but in an emergency, use a strong fish-landing net. To handle, back the goose into a corner and grasp her by the neck at the back of the head. When the wings are secured, slide one hand under her breast and grab her legs, keeping her head gently under your arm, so both the angry end and the messy end are well away from you. And remember, panic breeds panic. Geese are pretty unbiddable, but can be herded with long sticks.

Ganders' friendliness varies hugely and they should always be approached with care. Stand still if you're accosted, then move slowly forwards, or backwards. Always move unhurriedly

TIMELY ADVICE

Start feeding wild birds, well away from your poultry.

An annual bonfire gets rid of garden rubbish.

Raise containers off the ground and cover frost-vulnerable ones with bubble wrap.

Plant tulips in pots or in rows 20cm deep in the cutting garden. Cover if there are squirrels.

Spring pullets may start to lay for the first time and older hens will stop laying.

Prepare poultry houses and runs for winter and let birds into the dormant garden.

Tidy your pig-sties ready for next year's occupants.

Pick up any nuts as you find them and leave them to dry in nets or on trays in a dry spot.

among your flock, talking in a reassuring way. Watch their wings, and when they nip – they twist. It can be hard to tame goslings that have protective parents, but persevere; I've heard lots of charming stories about friendly geese, and Rosemary has kept them since she was 10 years old.

Pumpkin Soup with Roast Pumpkin Seeds and Walnut Pesto

A QUICK AND EASY SOUP that keeps away chills. I use up a small Crown Prince pumpkin that has spent time in my porch, welcoming visitors.

Preheat the oven to 180°C/gas 4.

Cut your pumpkin into quarters and scrape out the seeds.

Place the quarters on a baking tray, drizzle with olive oil and bake in the oven with 2 half onions until soft.

Remove from the oven, scoop out the flesh and blitz with the onions.

Dilute with stock to your preferred consistency, and warm.

Roast your own pumpkin seeds if you like: remove any flesh, wash thoroughly, spread evenly on a tray and bake in the same oven for 10 minutes (you'll have to de-husk them, unless you like them really crunchy). Alternatively, fry bought seeds in a pan with spices, salt and olive oil.

Serve the soup sprinkled with seeds and a spoonful of pesto made from a sprig of basil, a tablespoon of crushed walnuts, some salt and olive oil.

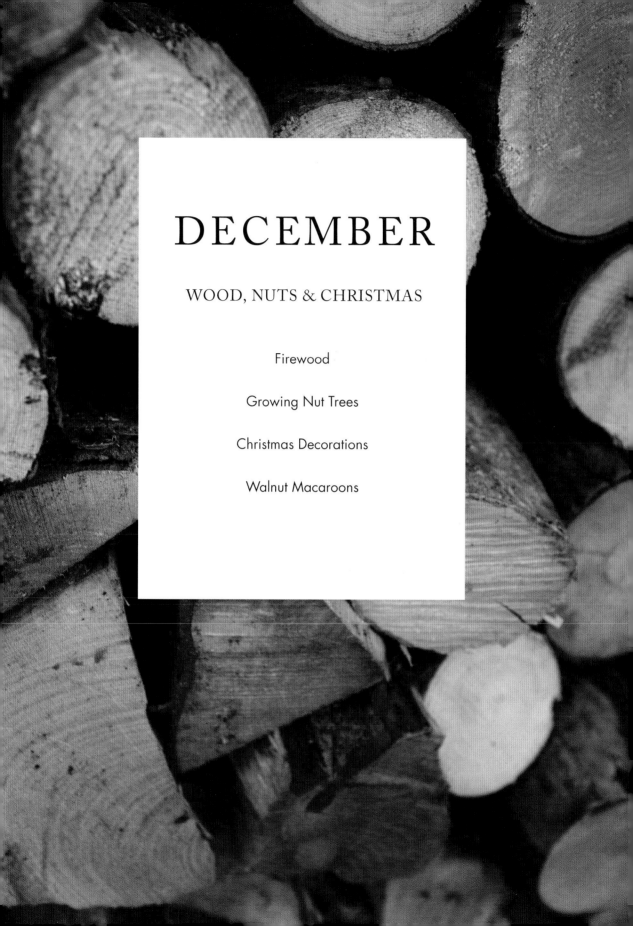

DECEMBER

WOOD, NUTS & CHRISTMAS

Firewood

Growing Nut Trees

Christmas Decorations

Walnut Macaroons

The winter garden continues
to provide a bounty.

Just count the homegrown elements that make up your Christmas dinner. From the traditional vegetables – red cabbage, Brussels sprouts, root vegetables and potatoes – to the herbs that enhance your gravy, the bay leaves that flavour your bread sauce and the rosemary that'll perk up the bird, perhaps even the bird itself – a home-raised capon, drake or gander? And maybe some home-cured bacon and sausages?

There'll be garden-grown nuts in petits-fours to pass round after the meal, or in roast chestnut stuffing or for spiced nuts; perhaps preserved fruits in brandy or fruit-flavoured gins and liqueurs, a medlar jelly to go with the bird or a chopped quince in your stuffing? A few pickles, dill-flavoured gherkins with your smoked fish

or creamy home-laid eggs in your *oeufs* Benedict? Or goose fat that you cook your roast spuds in? Now's the time to show off your garden's bounty.

December usually passes in a busy flash of preparations, celebrations, then recuperation. And while I try not to have too much evidence of Christmas on display before the 24th, the whole of Advent is a routine of decorating and cooking rituals that seem to take up the entire month.

Every year I try to slim down the festive elements, but my sons and their families get very grumpy if we don't go the whole hog. Even during years when we're reduced in numbers because of other family commitments, the remaining few expect their childhood Christmases to be replicated in detail.

I've tried bringing in whitened fig branches, stylish driftwood and even a woven willow tree, but nothing, in their minds, beats a real tree. We've tried growing conifers in pots and bringing them into the house for a few days, but they rarely survive – it's the dry summers that get them in the end.

I have a little more leeway with wreaths, tree decorations, garlands and bunting. I love experimenting with bits and bobs from the garden. Most seed heads, dried flowers, leaves, feathers, grasses, climbers, berries, fruits, veg and herbs have been tried in one way or another. Some more successfully than others, but it doesn't matter – their moment on stage is short and sweet.

A word of warning – all these elements are supremely flammable, and combined with festive candles can be incendiary. Never leave candles unsupervised – my first coherent childhood memory is being led away at kindergarten as the whole Christmas tree went up in smoke.

There's nothing nicer than sitting in front of a crackling fire after a day's work out in the winter garden. While most gardens won't supply enough wood for more than a few days' burning, there are lots of ways we can supplement our fuel needs and get a warm glow.

Firewood

Few of us will have the space to grow enough fast-growing trees like willow, alder, hawthorn or ash to completely supply our own needs, but by careful cutting, using a coppice rotation method, some could provide a log-shed full; and everyone gets the odd windblown casualty or major prunings that can be burnt.

Like wine, firewood needs to be laid down and seasoned. Green wood is full of water and needs to be dried out before burning. While hardwoods like oak, maple, fruitwoods and hawthorn take a couple of years before they're ready to burn, softwoods like pine and birch dry more quickly, though they spit and create fumes (some pines create deposits in your flue), and make good kindling. All species of wood contain a similar amount of energy per kilogram. The difference is the density of the wood, so because oak is twice as dense as pine, you'll need twice the volume to produce the same heat.

Chop and split firewood to increase its surface area and speed up drying. Store your firewood on an old pallet under cover that allows maximum airflow. I have two log piles, one in the front garden for easy delivery, made of pallets covered with leftover onduline roofing panels, and another under a seat by the oak tree in the back garden, near where the boughs fall.

Birch and beech rot easily and rotten wood creates little heat, so take extra care that these woods are kept dry. Ash has less moisture and can be burned undried. Sweet chestnut and willow spit a lot, but are fine in a wood-burning stove. Oak makes the best firewood when dry.

Kindling

The most effective kindling twigs are beech, hazel, ash, cedar or pine, as long as they are all bone dry. Save any prunings you make throughout the year, and if you have a hawthorn hedge, strip off the leaves and save after cutting. I dry my bay and lavender hedge trimmings with the leaves still on, and they start Christmas fires with a gorgeous smell. After every storm, large trees are a good source of windfall kindling, and the dry bark often found at the bottom of the woodpile burns well too.

Firelighters

I use dried cardoon seed heads, leek flowers, teasels, grass plumes, large thistle heads like the ones from the Scottish grey thistle or Our Lady's milkweed (*Silybum marianum*) – though the hens really love the seeds, so remove those first. All the various pine cones can be dipped in wax to make fabulously decorative fire starters, and beech mast and nutshells burn well too. At a loss for natural firelighters? Then roll newspaper inside a cardboard loo-roll holder.

Flavours

Whether on a campfire or an outdoor wood burner, everything tastes better cooked outside, and even mid-winter celebrations outside are fun if you're well wrapped up. Burn the endless supply of prunings and small wood that most gardens provide. I love the different flavours you get from wood cooking. Try grilling salmon on alder wood; apple and cherry are mild and good with poultry; burn maple with ham and oak with beef; but don't cook with pine or any wood that has been tanalised or treated with preservative. Herb prunings are particularly flavourful and full of volatile oils, as are old fennel stems.

Wood Ash

Ash from open fires and wood-burning stoves is useful mixed with other elements in the compost heap every foot or so, providing an alkaline mulch which will be useful under most soft fruit (except raspberries, which prefer an acid soil). Scatter it directly on to the soil in the veg garden in late winter, and fork in. It's beneficial for brassicas but not for potatoes. High in potassium, this leaches out if allowed to get wet. Wear a mask if you're dealing with wood ash, as it's not good for the chest.

I also mix wood ash with light garden soil and sandpit sand in the dust bath for my hens. I've boarded the area under the hen house where the soil is kept dry for the birds to dust bathe in.

ESSENTIAL VEG

If you have a windowsill or indoor grow light you can grow micro greens for winter salads. It's a good way to use up any leftover veg seeds too, or buy pulses and herb seeds as cooking ingredients – much cheaper than packets of seeds to sow.

- Try salad crops, leafy herbs, or pea and bean shoots.
- Sow thickly in plastic seed trays full of damp compost.
- Water lightly and your seedlings will be ready to eat in a few weeks.
- Snip off leaves with a pair of sharp kitchen scissors and eat straight away.

Growing Nut Trees

NUTS ARE A PRODUCTIVE BUNCH, a generous source of protein, and you can grow walnuts, hazels and chestnuts easily in the UK. Almonds are possible in the warmest corners. Planted in the depths of winter, these are trees of great beauty and versatility, but unfortunately the local wildlife think so too, so it is a battle with squirrelly hordes each year as to who benefits most from their copious harvest. Autumn in a nutshell.

Walnuts

The English or Persian walnut (*Juglans regia*) takes a lifetime to mature, but modern varieties like 'Lara', 'Franquette' and 'Broadview' take just a few years to establish. It is a beautiful tree that needs plenty of space. Nothing grows well under its leaves, though their smell, described by food historian Dorothy Hartley as 'a warm and pleasant smell, like the colour of a Persian carpet', is divine, and they were used in pot-pourris, especially in libraries.

Walnuts can be eaten 'wet' but most are dried on racks, then kept in a dry and airy spot. Eat them spiced, fried in butter with chopped rosemary or in olive oil with ras el hanout spice mix, or in home-made muesli with grated pear.

Hazel

Corylus avellana is the hedgerow nut of Britain. Whole families used to go nutting together, and their bounty was used in cakes, biscuits and in scrumptious praline, cooked in sugar at a low heat. Their catkins are the harbingers of spring, an early meal for pollinators; and the nuts, resting in pretty pale green or purple cases, are best picked when dry, but sometimes flavour has to be compromised by harvesting early to win the annual battle with wood mice.

Hazel prunings make great pea-stick plant supports. Regular coppicing by a third (said to improve the nut harvest) provides essential bean supports, arches and a framework to train fruit trees on.

Sweet Chestnuts

Castanea sativa, with figured cross-hatched bark, deeply toothed leaves and spiny burred nut cases, deserves pride of place in any garden. Best planted bare-rooted in early spring in well-drained fertile soil, it flowers with long catkins in July. The nuts are ready in October.

Chestnut flour is used to thicken soups in France, and chestnut purée, blended with mascarpone or cream, makes a lovely Yuletide cake filling. And there's nothing better than chestnuts eaten roasted in a pan on an open fire.

Almonds

Plant the varieties 'Ingrid', 'Robijn' or 'Princess', best grown as espaliers on a sheltered south-facing wall. Keep away from cross-pollination with peaches, otherwise your nuts will taste bitter. Encourage bumblebees into your garden – they'll forage early in their warm furry coats and pollinate the fragrant pink blossom.

Sweet-smelling twigs should be saved for kindling. Commercially, almonds are harvested on to tarpaulins spread on the ground by banging the boughs with a long pole and wearing protective headgear. Once most of the hulls have split, remove and place the nuts on a rack to dry.

Christmas Decorations

DECKING THE HALLS with the bounty from your garden is one of the most wonderful ways to create a unique family Christmas.

Wreaths

Every house should have a wreath to welcome visitors. A weather-proof porch makes a sheltered spot to hang delicate creations, and you won't have to rely on hardy evergreens. I like to use pressed leaves, and over the years must have made hundreds, using colourful leaves that have tempted me, or combinations I've admired in other people's gardens. I stick them with a glue-gun onto wire wreath frames from florist supply shops, but you could use a circlet of twining climbers or even cardboard.

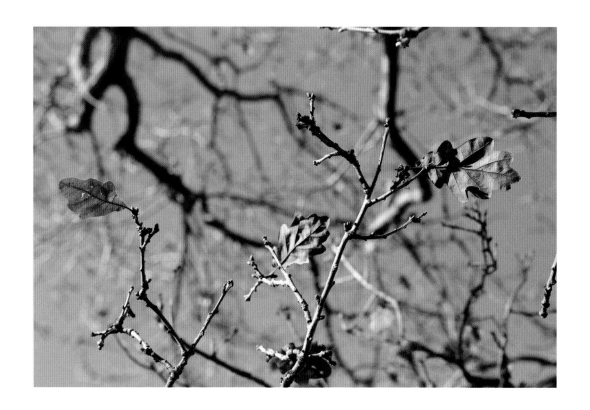

Garlands

Measure a length of pretty string, ribbon or wire the length of the doorway, mantelpiece or banister you want to decorate. Make loops at either end. Fold the string in half to find the centre and attach any pretty seed heads, dried fruit, leaves or feathers, spacing them evenly along its length. I've used dried cardoon buds, sprayed with glitz, and attached them along the French window that leads out to the garden.

Lanterns

A brilliant idea pinched from my grandson's nursery that makes a sweet lantern (see opposite). Take a few dried leaves from your cache under the mat (see page 114) – I used a fern. Find a pot lid of approximately 10cm diameter and roll a piece of tracing paper into a tube that fits your pot lid. Stick the dried leaves on to the tracing paper with spray-on glue, and sellotape the paper to make a tube. Pop in a tea light, or to be on the safe side, use a battery-operated one.

Leaf Name Tags

Use thick, substantial dried leaves, like oak or sycamore, and write the recipient's name with felt tip pen – gold always looks good. Tuck into the ribbon or stick to the parcel with a blob of glue. Some leaves will take a hole punch and can then be tied on to their parcel with a bit of glittery wire or ribbon.

Table Rings

A herb ring graces our kitchen table and means we have an instant supply of sprigs of herbs to hand. I use an old bundt tin I found at a car boot sale. The candle is placed in the central well, and little bunches of winter herbs are added round the outside. A circlet of houseleeks, flowering bulbs or fresh flowers would look good too, and this year I used dried blue echinops globes.

TIMELY ADVICE

Order the new season's seed catalogues.

Support some of the smaller companies that actually produce their own seed.

Alternatively, resolve to save your own seed.

Check your stock's water hasn't frozen over during frosty days.

Watch to see if pots of bulbs are sprouting, and bring them into the house.

Strain jars of fruit preserved in alcohol and decant into bottles. The boozy fruit can be saved and served with cream for a festive pudding.

Walnut Macaroons

THESE ARE RUSTIC chewy biscuits that could be made with almonds or hazelnuts as well. Dip some in melted chocolate and sprinkle with sea salt – I've gilded mine. They'll keep for a couple of weeks in an airtight tin, and make good Christmas presents, packed in a pretty box tied with ribbon.

Preheat your oven to 150°C/gas 2.

Arrange sheets of rice paper on two baking trays.

Whisk 3 egg whites until really stiff, then gradually add 80g of caster sugar.

Fold in 100g of ground walnuts, then drop the mixture on to the rice paper using two spoons.

Top each biscuit with a whole nut and bake for 30 minutes.

Gild, following the product instructions.

Useful Websites

COMPOST
Carbongold.com to improve soil nutrition.

Dorsetcharcoal.co.uk – locally produced organic soil conditioner.

Hotbincomposting.com for aerobic composting.

Bokashi system composters from wigglywigglers.co.uk.

Wormeries from wormcity.co.uk.

SEEDS
Realseeds.co.uk for heirloom veg seeds chosen for home gardeners.

Seedsofitaly.com – salad and veg seeds in generous packets.

Use ethicalconsumer.org or their print magazine to find the most ethical seeds and composts.

Organiccatalogue.com for organic and environmentally friendly products.

CAR BOOT SALES
To find a boot sale near you try carbootsales.org and carbootjunction.com.

For antique and junk fairs: iacf.co.uk and antique-atlas.com.

DUCKS
The Domestic Waterfowl Club of Great Britain: domestic-waterfowl.co.uk.

The British Call Duck Club: britishcallduckclub.org.uk.

Marriages Poultry Feed for info about poultry feed: marriages.co.uk.

AllenandPage.com for a range of feeds approved by The Vegetarian Society.

For tips to prevent rats, see bpca.org.uk.

POLLINATORS
Biobees.com for information about natural beekeeping.

Naturalbeekeepingtrust.org – new directions in bee-centred beekeeping.

Plantlife.org.uk – saving wild plants and their habitats.

Beebristol.org for conservation and raising awareness.

Your local wildlife trust at wildlifetrusts.org.

QUAILS & GUINEA FOWL
Quailfarm.co.uk – all about Japanese Quail.

Guinea-fowl.co.uk – a useful website devoted to guinea fowl.

HENS
Chickenvet.co.uk – for your nearest vet, medicines and products.

Housing, supplies and feed from flytesofancy.co.uk.

Poultryclub.org – for pure breeders lists.

Henkeepersassociation.co.uk – online advice for those who keep poultry for pleasure.

The Battery Hen Welfare Trust finds homes for ex-battery hens – bhwt.org.uk.

HERBS
Herbsociety.org.uk – herb education society.

Jekkasherbfarm.com – online catalogue of organic herbs.

Invictaherbs.co.uk – specialist growers of culinary herbs.

CUT FLOWERS
Haxnicks.co.uk for garden care and plant protection.

Gee-tee.co.uk for a good range of bulbs.

Auriculas.org.uk for information about the history and showing of auriculas.

Johnsonssweetpeas.co.uk is a grower and
supplier of sweet pea seeds and plants.
Wandmsmith.co.uk – florists suppliers.

BERRIES

Lubera.co.uk – breeders and growers of unusual
berries and fruits.
Cherry Aid Branch Wraps to protect your trees
from birds – cherrynets.co.uk.
Pomonafruits.co.uk are soft fruit specialists.
Ashridgetrees.co.uk sell white alpine strawberry
plants.
Niwaki.com for fruit picking ladders and
pruning tools.

SNAILS

Hrh-escargots.co.uk sell snail growing kits and
give courses.

STONE FRUITS

Bernwodeplants.co.uk for historic and
traditional stone-fruit trees.
Brogdaleonline.co.uk – specialist fruit tree centre.

ORCHARD FRUITS

Orangepippintrees.co.uk for information about
varieties and orchards.
Walcotnursery.co.uk for organic fruit trees.

SALADS

Rocketgardens.co.uk deliver boxes of veg plug
plants.
Organicplants.co.uk – a good selection of
organic veg plants.

MUSHROOMS

Merryhill-mushrooms.co.uk for grow-your-own
mushroom kits.
Gourmetmushrooms.co.uk for many varieties of
mushroom spawn to grow at home.

PIGS

Defra.gov.uk for information about keeping
pigs.
To find your local Trading Standards office:
www.gov.uk/find-local-trading-standards
-office.
Britishpigs.org.uk to find breeders in your area.
The Rare Breeds Survival Trust: rbst.org.uk.
Doddingtonplacegardens.co.uk is a lovely garden
with home raised pigs.
Samphireshop.co.uk sells pork products from
their smallholding.
Suppliesforsmallholders.co.uk for pig and
poultry items.

GEESE

Waterfowl.org.uk for keepers of wild and
domestic waterfowl.
Gooseclub.org.uk open to anyone interested in
domestic geese.
Electricfencing.co.uk for the right fencing
solution for your animals and birds.

NUTS

For almond, chestnut and walnut trees –
walnuttrees.co.uk.
Kentishcobnuts.com for varieties and
information.
Otterfarm.co.uk for plot-to-plate courses and
nut trees.

WOOD

Grow your own firewood – thewillowbank.com.

Index

About the Author

Gardening productively is one of Francine Raymond's greatest pleasures, heightened by the chance to chronicle her experiences in a dozen or so books; newspapers, including a six-year weekly column in the *Telegraph*); magazines such as *The English Garden*, *Country Living*, *Gardens Illustrated* and the general poultry press; and on her blog at kitchen-garden-hens.co.uk.

After a lifetime on an acre in Suffolk, populated with hens and ducks, Francine now gardens a small town plot by the sea in Whitstable with the help of her grandsons and a few bantams.

She started her career as a fashion designer, moving to Milan in the seventies and returned to an abiding love – the English countryside – with her small children. Making the most of her plot, Francine opened her garden to the public – an evangelist, hoping to prove that a productive garden can be both stylish and a source of healthy food: a delight to all the senses.

Thanks

Thank you, Sarah for recording my efforts so beautifully and Friederike for displaying them to such great advantage: my garden and its occupants have never looked so glamorous. Thank you, Rose for having the vision and faith to commission this book, and to Lucy for seeing it through. It has been a pleasure to work with you all on such a lovely project.

Author photograph by
Charlie Colmer

1 3 5 7 9 10 8 6 4 2

Square Peg, an imprint of Vintage,
20 Vauxhall Bridge Road,
London SW1V 2SA

Square Peg is part of the Penguin Random House
group of companies whose addresses can be
found at global.penguinrandomhouse.com.

Penguin
Random House
UK

First published by Square Peg in 2017

Penguin.co.uk/vintage

A CIP catalogue record for this book is available
from the British Library

ISBN 9781910931325

Design by Friederike Huber
Photography by Sarah Cuttle

Printed and bound by Toppan Leefung Printing Ltd

Penguin Random House is committed to a
sustainable future for our business, our readers
and our planet. This book is made from Forest
Stewardship Council® certified paper.

MIX
Paper from
responsible sources
FSC® C018179